LESSONS IN LOVING

Annie Carter

Lessons in Loving
© 2019 Annie Carter
All rights reserved.
Printed in the United States of America
ISBN: 978-0-578-53740-5

In memory of
Moses and Maggie McCall

CHAPTER ONE

Maggie, a young African American woman, settled back in her seat. Her five-month-old John nestled snugly in her arms. Her other two children, Annie Ruth, two and a half and Dorothy, one and a half, sat in the seats across from her. A middle aged Black woman occupied the seat beside her.

It was quiet in the lone railroad car. The car was filled with people dozing, half awake, as the train sped through the night. Each person had their own dreams of what the future held for them. Moses had sent money to Maggie so that she and the rest of his growing family could join him in MT. Union, PA, where he had found a job at General Refractories, a plant where he worked making silica bricks for the various steel mills in the surrounding areas.

Twenty-four-year-old Maggie, an optimist by choice, had had no doubts that Moses would send for his family as soon as he could; he had always done what he said he would do in the five years that she had known him, and she had no reason to doubt him now. He was a 31-year-old African American man. A hard worker from a good family of sharecroppers in the town where Maggie lived with her parents.

Maggie was looking forward to a good life up North. She knew that things would be tough at first. The family would live with Moses' first cousin, Riley and her family of six in a single family house. The five in Maggie's family would all share one bedroom. Hopefully this situation would not last long and Maggie and Moses would find a residence of their own.

All of these thoughts flashed through Maggie's mind as she sat in the train car watching over her three children. They had boarded the train at 10pm so the children were asleep as the time approached 3am. Her mother-in-law had fixed a shoe box of fried chicken and cake. This, Maggie and the two girls would eat in the early morning. John, the baby, would be breast fed when he awoke. Hopefully the lady sitting beside Maggie would watch John while Maggie took the girls to the bathroom. The lady seemed pleasant enough and had talked to Maggie briefly before falling asleep herself. One thing she said had kind of put Maggie off. She implied that Maggie was "running after your husband." Maggie had nicely but firmly told her that her husband had "sent for" her. In her mind she had "put the lady in her place." Oh well, at least she had offered to help Maggie with the children. She wasn't all bad even if she did jump to conclusions, the wrong ones at that!

Before Maggie knew it, the sun was coming up and John was beginning to squirm in Maggie's arms. She changed him and was able to breast feed him before her two daughters awakened. This they did, around 8am. Maggie took them to the bathroom and then fed them. Just before 10:15am Maggie got the girls and John into their snowsuits, as the train was due in MT Union at 10:35am. They all made their way to the front of the car where the conductor told Maggie to go. The train slowly came to a stop. The conductor helped Maggie and her family off the train and placed the large suitcase on the platform. Maggie looked around. There was not a soul to be seen. The platform was deserted. Maggie had no choice but to stand still and wait. She looked down the platform. Way down at the end she saw a tall man and a much shorter woman. Thank God, it was Moses and his cousin, Riley. She was never so glad to see two people in her life!

CHAPTER TWO

Moses woke up with great anticipation on this bright cold day in February 1940. It was noisy in his cousin's house as her children got ready for school. Usually Moses was himself up and gone to work at the brick manufacturing plant. When he left South Carolina in November 1938, he came to Claysburg, PA where he hoped to find employment at the plant there with his brothers. Unfortunately, that plant was not hiring, so Moses had come to MT Union where the same company had a plant. Moses got a job there and as soon as he got a paycheck, he sent money to his wife, Maggie, so that she and their three children could join him. This was the day that they were coming and Moses was anxious to get up, eat his breakfast, and get to the train station to meet them. Sadly, he did not have good news for Maggie: during the two week since he had sent her the money to come, he had been laid off. Nevertheless, it would be good to see his family.

Soon Moses and Riley set off for the station. They did not want to be late because it would be hard for Maggie to manage the three children and the luggage. The train was due to arrive at 10:35am. It was now 10:15am so Moses being six feet tall and lanky had to remind himself not to walk too fast for his five foot, four inch cousin. As they neared the station they saw the train come in, briefly stop, and take off. They knew his family was there. The station sat on an overhead platform. They rushed up the steps and reaching the top, they saw Maggie and the three kids on the platform. They rushed to them, Moses gave Maggie a quick hug and took John, the baby, from her. He greeted their two daughters, Annie Ruth, and Dorothy. Then they all started for Riley's house. Moses was overjoyed that his family had finally arrived. Even though he was presently not working he knew that he and Maggie would somehow make it together in their new location. They were in the North. That surely held more promise for them than the cotton fields of the South! They looked forward to their future with much anticipation.

CHAPTER THREE

Annie and Dorothy were in the hallway outside of the room that they shared with their mother, father, and brother, in Cousin Riley's house. They could tell that something was going on. Their mother seemed very upset and their father was trying to calm her down. Annie was quiet. She knew that her mother was upset and she was determined not to bother her. Her sister, Dorothy, however, had let the whole thing upset her and she was crying. Annie thought to herself that her sister should grow up and stop crying about every little thing. When was she going to realize that crying did not help? She was such a baby.

Annie and Dorothy were too young to know that their parents had been to the doctor's office. Their parents learned that Maggie had had a miscarriage and that was the reason that their mother was upset. Maggie and the three children had just been up North for two months. Their father had been called back to work shortly after their arrival. Now he and Maggie were saving money so that they could move to their own house or apartment. Cousin Riley was not rushing them to move but they knew that it was an inconvenience for them to be there. So they had been looking for their own quarters. Maggie took the kids to the park every day to give Cousin Riley some space to be with her own children. The four bedroom house was bursting at the seams with Cousin Riley, Cousin George and their six children. The sooner the Moses McCall family could move out the better it would be for all of them.

CHAPTER FOUR

Moses, Maggie, and their three children had been in their own apartment for four months now. Moses was working steadily. He awakened every morning at six, ate his breakfast and left the house shortly thereafter and was at the plant by seven. Maggie prepared his lunch the night before. This enabled her to sleep for another half hour before rising to get the children fed and dressed for the day. She had not told Moses yet but she was sure that she was pregnant. She would soon tell him so he could stop by the doctor's office to make an appointment for her so that she could be certain, and also to begin prenatal care.

There was only one African American doctor in town and most of the African Americans went to him when they needed medical care. His office was in his house, a large two story brick building which he shared with his wife. They had no children. When any of the children had serious illnesses, Maggie took them to Dr. Brooks. He also gave the children their immunizations when they were needed. Along with the pastors of the three African American churches in town, Dr. Brooks was the only other professional. Dr. Brooks attended no church however. He and his wife kept mostly to themselves. His wife could be seen sitting on the porch in their swing on most days. She did not socialize with any of the African American women in town and seemed to lead a solitary existence. Little was known about the couple except that they were from Virginia.

Moses and Maggie had been lucky to find an apartment in a two-story house which had been converted into two apartments. They lived in the upstairs apartment while a single white widower lived in the downstairs apartment. Except for brief greetings between them, Moses and Maggie had nothing to do with Mr. Fred as he was called. He worked at another of the brick manufacturing plants in town.

Mr. Fred was no kind of a housekeeper. The same tattered curtains could be seen hanging from his windows as had been hanging there when his wife died. He had no visitors. His life consisted of going to work and coming home. He must have had a drinking problem because sometimes he could be seen staggering home.

Unlike Mr. Fred, Maggie kept their apartment very clean. Each spring she cleaned the apartment from top to bottom, taking down curtains, washing them, and putting them back up. Their apartment consisted of a kitchen, living room, and one large bedroom where all of the family slept.

One day while Maggie was cleaning the bedroom, Annie Ruth saw dirty dishes in the sink. She decided that she and Dorothy, who was now called Dot, would wash them. So, pulling the step stool over to the sink, that was what she did. She didn't realize that the sink was running over and getting water on the floor. When Maggie was finished in the bedroom, she came to the kitchen and found a big mess. She did not like it at all, but didn't punish Annie Ruth too severely as she knew she was trying to help.

CHAPTER FIVE

Maggie lay on three kitchen chairs which she had put together in the kitchen. Her children gathered at the door, looking at her, wondering what was the matter. They saw that there was water on the floor and that their mother was in some distress. Maggie, for her part, was just hoping that her husband got home and went for Dr. Brooks. They had no telephone and there was no one else Maggie could send for him. She knew if she lay quietly the pains would not increase. She and Moses had notified his relatives in Claysburg PA of Maggie's condition and they had arranged for her sister-in-law to come to help her when the baby was born. Ida, the sister-in-law, was coming the next day. If Maggie could make it through the next few hours everything would be okay.

About one half hour later she heard Moses open the downstairs door and gave a sigh of relief; now Moses could get the doctor and Maggie could get on with having their fourth child.

Aunt Ida, as the kids called her, came the next day. They liked Aunt Ida. She was always cheerful and laughed a lot, Moses and Maggie let Aunt Ida name their new baby – a girl. She named her Helaine Marie. Annie Ruth thought that Dr. Brooks had brought the baby with him when he came. How else could one explain how one minute there was no baby and the next minute there was a crying baby. Moses and Maggie said nothing to enlighten Annie Ruth. Dot and J.D. (as John was now called) were too young to express any thoughts one way or another. They all looked at their new sister in awe. They wondered why she slept all the time. She slept in the bed between their mother and father. Annie Ruth hoped they would not roll over and smash her to death. She was so tiny. Maggie breast fed her as she had done the others before her.

Soon Helaine was able to crawl around on the floor. The other kids liked to play with her. They always had a good time together, playing with the few toys that their parents could afford to buy them. The important thing was that they felt loved and wanted, snug in their upstairs apartment with their parents.

With their family growing, Moses and Maggie began looking around for bigger quarters. When one half of the duplex next door became available they decided to rent it. Downstairs, it had a kitchen, hallway and living room. Upstairs there were 3 bedrooms. There was no bathroom, only an outhouse in the back of the large lot in the back of the duplex. The only running water was at the sink in the kitchen. For heat, there was a coal stove in the kitchen and one in the living room. Cooking was done on a kerosene stove in the kitchen.

Upstairs, the girls shared one bedroom and the boys the other. Moses and Maggie and the current baby slept in the third bedroom. Shortly after moving into the duplex, in 1943, their fifth child, a boy, whom they named Benjamin Melvin, arrived. Although Annie Ruth went to school and was in the first grade, she still thought that Dr. Brooks brought the baby with him when he came.

CHAPTER SIX

Life settled into a pattern for the Moses and Maggie McCall family. Moses worked every day except Saturday and Sunday. Maggie stayed home and took care of the children. On Fridays, Moses came home, got dressed and went out. This pattern had been invented in the South when everybody worked in the fields all week, including one half day on Saturday, came home Saturday afternoon, got dressed and went to "Town" Saturday afternoon into the evening. For the men, going to town included smoking and drinking. Since Moses had had to quit school in the third grade to help on the share-cropping farm, he had gotten into this habit at an early age. As he got older, his drinking got worse and created problems between Moses and Maggie, as Moses only wanted to discuss any problems they might have when he was drinking. Therefore, they had many fights on Friday and Saturday evenings after Moses had been out drinking. Sometimes the children ended up crying, begging them to stop. There is much debate as to what causes alcoholism, heredity or the environment. Many Native Americans suffer from alcoholism. Moses' maternal grandmother was full-blooded Cherokee. Whatever the cause, it was becoming a problem for this family.

Moses may have been out drinking on Friday and Saturday nights but on Monday morning he was ready to meet the man and did just that. He now had seven mouths to feed and he took that very seriously. During the week, he was a good husband and father.

LESSONS IN LOVING

The whole family sat down and ate together every evening. The conversation included everyone. Moses and Maggie encouraged all their children to join in, and meal times were extremely pleasant. After supper, as the evening meal was called, everyone congregated in the kitchen. The kids did their homework. Moses tried to read the newspaper. Since he had had to stop school in the third grade he could not read nor write. He learned to do so at the same time as his children did. As they sat doing their homework, Moses would spell words from the newspaper. No one even thought of laughing about it and dutifully told him what the words were.

CHAPTER SEVEN

Maggie and the children attended church every Sunday at MT Hope Missionary Baptist Church which was down the street from where they lived. Moses attended occasionally. The children attended Sunday School as they got old enough to walk down the street by themselves. As they got older, Maggie began to sing in the Choir. She had a beautiful voice and often sang solos. In 1945, she was hospitalized for the birth of their sixth child, Mary Janelle. She came home raving about the nurse who had taken care of her. From that day on, her oldest child, Annie Ruth decided that she was going to become a nurse so she too could help people. The nurse, whose name was Janelle, never knew the effect she had on Annie Ruth. Maggie, however, knew that Annie Ruth would never be the same. She quietly nourished Annie Ruth's dream because she knew from experience that what Annie learned, she also passed on to her sisters and brothers.

CHAPTER EIGHT

Annie was going to school! On the first day of school, Maggie got the kids up early, dressed and fed them, taking care of Annie's hair especially. She asked the elderly lady next door to watch the rest of her brood so she could walk with Annie to her new school. She had previously taken Annie's immunization record and her birth certificate to the school office and now she was anxious to meet Annie's first grade teacher. Maggie had only been able to go to school through tenth grade. Education was very important to her and she wanted to make sure Annie got off to a good start. She knew that Annie was smart; she had started teaching Annie her numbers and she loved learning. Annie loved to teach her younger siblings anything she learned, thus Maggie had more than one reason to gently push her daughter in that area. Annie was a quiet dutiful little girl and she tried her best to please her mother in any way that she could. After meeting her first grade teacher, Annie sat quietly at a long table with six of her classmates. She was a little nervous about the school situation, but she loved new things and had high hopes that she would have a good time. All of her classmates were white, except for one African American boy who sat beside her. Sammy Green was his name and he was also quiet. As the days went on Annie and Sammy became good friends. One thing though, Sammy loved to copy off Annie's paper. When she learned to write her name, Sammy at first wrote his name correctly. But when Annie's mother taught her to include her middle name, Ruth, Sammy looked at her paper and wrote Samuel Ruth Green. Annie thought it was funny and laughed about it. She told her brothers and sisters about it when she went home. Her mother smiled when she heard the story. Annie was a natural born leader.

CHAPTER NINE

Annie loved school but she did not like recess. The other children did not like Annie and Sammy. They would not play with them. They were always last to be called to kick the ball when the kids played "kick ball". They were too young to know why but thought that it was not fair. It made them angry. When it was their time to kick the ball Annie and Sammy got rid of their anger by putting all of their might into kicking the ball. That way they could put their full attention to their school work when they went back inside.

Every day when Annie came home from school Maggie sat her down in the kitchen and put Ben, the baby, in her arms and let her feed him while she prepared the evening meal. Annie enjoyed holding her brother and feeding him. She felt very grown up that her mother would let her do this. After supper Maggie helped her with her homework. Sometimes all the kids gathered around Moses and he would tell them stories about growing up in the South. One story that he told about his little brother, who died, always made him cry. He said his little brother was sick a long time and every day, when he came in from picking cotton in the fields, he would talk to his brother and they planned things to do when he got well. The little brother loved his big brother. He called him Bubba, a name given to the oldest son in families in the South. It was the shortened name for Brother. Sadly, Moses' little brother did not get well and died. Moses always started to cry when he told his children about his little brother. They knew that their father had a tender heart and they loved him for telling them this story. Any time that any of them were sick, they always got special treatment from their father. In a way, they were extensions of his little brother.

CHAPTER TEN

The situation between Moses and Maggie was getting progressively worse as the weeks wore on. Moses continued to drink on weekends and their fights escalated. Maggie was very distressed because she could see that the children were scared as the fights went on. Dot (as Dorothy was now called) had threatened Moses with her toy broom one Friday evening during one of their fights. Maggie knew she had to do something.

One Friday evening Maggie took the money Moses gave her and after packing everyone's clothes, bought train tickets to Philadelphia. She decided to go there to stay with her Aunt Fannie and her husband, Uncle Bob. Even though she had a 7 month old baby and four other children, she took this drastic step out of desperation over her home situation. When they arrived in Philadelphia, Aunt Fannie welcomed them with open arms and took the family into their home joyfully. She had two grown daughters of her own but made room for Maggie and her children.

Maggie enrolled Annie and Dot in the school around the corner on the following Monday. They went to the new school and it seemed that things would work out. The first day went okay. Annie and Dot came home for lunch and then at the end of the day. On the second day, Dot came home for lunch, but Annie did not. Annie took a wrong turn and got lost. She was standing on the street crying when a lady approached her. When the lady found out that she was lost, she took her to the police station. The police put Annie in their car and drove her around the neighborhood seeing if she recognized her Aunt's house. Annie could not identify where Aunt Fannie lived. The police took her back to the police station. As they were discussing their next step, the phone rang. It was Maggie calling to ask them if they had found Annie. Annie heard the police say, "Yes, she's here, crying her eyes out." Soon Maggie appeared to take Annie back to Aunt Fannie's house. That evening, Moses appeared. Needless to say Maggie was glad to see him. She packed all their clothes and they all returned to Mount Union with Moses. During the ensuing years, regardless of how bad the situation at home got, Maggie may have kept her suitcases packed, but she never left again. They even had three additional children: The aforementioned, Mary Janelle (Jan), born in June 1945; James Arthur (Jim), born in July 1948; and Gerald Eugene (Jerry), born in December 1951. Jerry changed his name to Mamadou Chinyelu late in his adulthood.

CHAPTER ELEVEN

As the children grew and there were more mouths to feed, Maggie worked for white families in the upper part of town. Although she was thrifty and spent money wisely, there never seemed to be enough. She bought a lot of beans, poultry and fish for her family and cooked well balanced meals. During the summer, she bought fresh fruits from farmers from the surrounding area and peeled and canned them so that they would last through the winter. She was an accomplished seamstress and her children always wore the latest styles. During the summer, Moses or Maggie would pull out the hand cranked ice cream maker, and make homemade ice cream.

The children all went to Sunday School, so that when Easter or Christmas rolled around, there would be poems or plays to learn for the different programs at the church which they attended. Maggie sang in the choir and went to rehearsals every Friday night. Annie Ruth was left in charge on these nights. The younger children listened to her when she told them to do something. They loved their big sister and knew that she loved them and that she would never tell them to do anything wrong. All in all, they were a big loving family although they did not have everything that other kids had, they did not feel that they were poor, which of course they were. Nevertheless, there was much laughter in the house-hold.

There were two times of the year that all the children looked forward to: These were Christmas and the Picnic. At Christmas time there were toys and gifts for everyone. There were special things to eat: cakes, pies, oranges, apples, nuts, etc. The house was all a glow with a Christmas tree and a wreath on the door. The young children all went to bed early on Christmas Eve and were up early to see what Santa Claus had brought them. Later there was a big turkey dinner with all the trimmings. The day was capped off with a special program at church, where the children wore the new clothing which they had received.

The Sunday School Picnic was held on the fourth Friday in July. All the African American churches from all the surrounding towns spent this day at a big amusement park in the area. Everybody got new clothes to wear. Maggie spent the day before the picnic preparing good things to eat. Maggie and the children rode to the Picnic on the Sunday School bus. Moses worked half a day and got a ride there with one of the men from where he worked. The younger kids spent all day on rides. The older children roller skated and swam. People, who had left town to find work in New York or Philadelphia, came back for the Picnic. A good time was had by all. The ride home was quiet. Everyone was tired from the full day of enjoying themselves at the amusement park.

CHAPTER TWELVE

Maggie was raised by her grandmother. She was the oldest of May's 10 children. May had three children before she was married. Although Maggie's father wanted to marry May, she refused. Maggie talked about her father to her children. She told them that she remembers that as a young child her father had sat her on his knee and told her that he was going away and would not see her again. She said he was very sad, and so was she.

Life at Maggie's grandmother's house was not a pleasant one. She said her grandmother was mean to her and that she said hurtful things to her. Maggie said that when she began developing breasts as an adolescent, her grandmother mocked her and said "Look at you. You're getting to be a woman. You are probably going to have a baby. Your stomach is going to get big and I am going to laugh and laugh at you." Maggie was angry, but said nothing. She said she was determined not to get pregnant and that she took a long piece of a cotton binder and bound her chest with it so that her breasts were not noticeable.

Maggie's main job was to watch her younger brother and sister, Johnny and Queenie. They had lots of fun together. They made her life bearable. Her mother finally got married, but lived in another town. The three of them went to live with their mother and her husband when Maggie was sixteen. Her mother continued to have children and had an additional seven. Maggie remembered how her grandmother had mocked her about getting pregnant and was determined not to. So, when she married Moses at age 20, she was still a virgin.

Moses was born into a large close knit family. His parents had a total of sixteen children. Moses was the oldest boy, therefore according to Southern traditions, he was nick named "Brother" which soon was shortened to Bubba. The first male was widely respected and revered by the other children. He was almost like a third parent, in that his brothers and sisters turned to him if their parents weren't available. Moses knew this and was very protective of his siblings. He looked after them in all the ways that a big brother should. They knew that if they had a problem, Bubba would help them in any way he could. When they reached adulthood most of them moved to a small town about fifty miles from where Moses and Maggie lived, Claysburg, Pennsylvania. About every few months a couple of car loads of them came to visit Moses and Maggie. They would spend all day Sunday eating and talking together. The children were always happy to see them because their uncles always gave them money. Their aunts gave them hugs and kisses. A good time was had by all.

When Moses' mother and father got too old to work the sharecroppers farm they too relocated to Claysburg to be near their children. They lived there during their old age. As they got sick and eventually died, they were funeralized in Claysburg and Morrisville, Pennsylvania. They were both taken back to South Carolina to be buried. The plant at which Moses 'brothers worked relocated to Morrisville in the early 1950's. They all relocated there following their source of employment. By this time there were many cousins, aunts and uncles living in Claysburg. They also moved to Morrisville. An eminent domain situation caused them all to have to move into Trenton, New Jersey right across the river from Morrisville.

CHAPTER THIRTEEN

Annie Ruth was in the fourth grade when she decided she was going to become a nurse. From then on, her mantra was, "I am going to become a nurse, marry a doctor, and have four kids." Annie believed she could become a registered nurse because there was an African American registered nurse who lived in Huntingdon, a small town twelve miles away from MT Union. This lady regularly came to MT Hope Missionary Baptist Church to speak. Most likely this nurse did not know that there was a little African American girl for whom she was a role model. But she was, and all of Annie's efforts from then on were directed towards becoming a nurse. She read stories about nurses. She did research to see what education was necessary to become a nurse. Her main goal was to become a nurse so she could help people the way nurse Janelle had helped Annie's mother when she was hospitalized to give birth to her sister, Janelle.

It was around this time also that Annie's Sunday School teachers noticed that she was very interested in learning about how she could become a Christian. They talked to Maggie about it and at the age of eleven, Annie was baptized, serving her Lord and Savior, Jesus Christ. When her brothers and sisters reached this approximate age they, too, became Christians. Annie didn't realize it, but just by living her life, she was a leader. That was just as well because otherwise, the responsibility would have been overbearing and too much on her young shoulders. Of course, Moses and

Maggie could see it and needless to say, they were happy to see that Annie was setting good examples for her siblings. Therefore, they encouraged her in any way that they could. At the same time there was some amount of sibling rivalry as Annie's brothers and sisters tried to live up to her examples. There was probably some resentment as well but Annie was too busy living her life to ever let it bother her. For the most part the Moses and Maggie McCall family was largely a big, happy one.

As the children got older they had chores to do at home.

They also did jobs outside the home to have spending money for extra things they needed. One of the boys had a paper route; another helped a neighbor in his landscape business. The older children got up early in the summer months to get on a truck, which went to surrounding farms, where they picked beans. As teenagers, the girls cleaned houses in the upper part of town for extra money. Moses told each of them that he would not take their money the way his father had taken his, but that they could spend their money for things they needed or wanted.

As the girls reached adolescence, Maggie took each aside and told them "the facts of life." She told them that men would kill for the need to have sex with them. She told them to wait until they were married to have sex, as she had. One of the daughters later would say that Maggie scared her to death. Ironically, the sisters did not discuss the matter between themselves at the time.

CHAPTER FOURTEEN

Annie was a quiet, reserved girl. When she saw people being done wrong though, she was not afraid to act. Joan was just one person that Annie saw being mistreated. Joan was new in town. Her father was the new minister at the Methodist Church. There was a story going around that Joan liked girls. She was always alone. Annie saw this and decided she would approach Joan. She began waiting for Joan and walking with her to school although Joan was two years ahead of Annie. Annie knew that she ran the risk of being gossiped about herself, but she never could stand by and see someone being mistreated. She continued to wait for Joan every day. Until one day, her father, Moses, told Annie that Joan was "too old" for her. Since Moses very rarely got involved in his girls' lives, Annie knew that he felt strongly about this and that most likely there were stories going around about her and Joan. Since Annie knew how her father felt about the situation, and since she did not want to cause him needless worry, Annie stopped waiting for Joan, even though the stories were false. Annie felt secure in her sexual orientation. She liked boys and at the time had a huge crush on Reggie who attended her church. He was attracted to Annie, also, and they talked to each other every chance they could. However, they both were so busy with school and their after school jobs that they had no chance to date. They both had definite plans for what they were going to do after they graduated from high school and were not that concerned about dating. Every time, when at parties they played "post office", Reggie would always try to guess Annie's number so that she had to go out on the porch to kiss him. They knew how the other one felt and were satisfied with what little contact they had in their young lives. They thought that later there would be plenty of time to develop their relationship, if that was what they wanted to do.

CHAPTER FIFTEEN

In seventh grade, Annie discovered the library! Her English teacher gave everyone an assignment to take out one book from the library and report on it. Annie chose Ethel Waters' autobiography, "His Eye is on the Sparrow." Annie took it home to read and read it through in two evenings. Unfortunately, she left it on the kitchen table and her baby brother, Jimmy, got it and tore one of its pages. Annie didn't know what to do. Should she just keep it or should she take it back? She was scared. She decided to take it back to the library and to say nothing to the librarian. Maybe she would not discover the torn page. But alas, Annie was in her second period class, when she saw the librarian at the door. Mrs. Jones, the librarian, asked the teacher if she could speak to Annie. So, shaking and afraid, Annie went outside the classroom. Mrs. Jones showed her the torn page and asked Annie what happened. Annie told her the truth. To her surprise, the librarian was not angry. She just told Annie to keep any further books that she took out of the library, out of the reach of her younger brothers and sisters. Annie was so relieved. Mrs. Jones' attitude opened up a whole new world for Annie. After that, she took out several books from the library each week. In the evening after supper and homework, Annie could be found sitting by the coal stove reading. Though the kitchen might be filled with other people talking and laughing, Annie was oblivious to them. She was worlds away with her head stuck in her book. Fortunately, Mrs. Jones had not reacted negatively to the torn page in the first book which Annie took out of the library. Mrs. Jones' attitude allowed a whole new experience for Annie, which would become a permanent part of her life.

CHAPTER SIXTEEN

Annie was flying at the top of a long dark tunnel going toward a bright white light. There were people standing there. Annie could not make out who they were, but she felt that she knew them. They seemed to be telling Annie to go back and that it was not her time, yet. One of the people walked toward Annie. At that time, she woke up. Annie kept having flashbacks of the above scene throughout her childhood. Maggie had told Annie about the time when she, at the age of one year, had a terrible coughing spell, and then went limp. They were living on a campground in South Carolina then. When Annie went limp, Maggie sent someone to call Moses, who was two doors down the road playing cards. When he came, Maggie implored him to get someone to take them to the doctor's office. Moses took one look at Annie's limp body and said, "It doesn't look like there is any need to take her to the doctor", meaning that Annie was too far gone for the doctor to do any good. But Maggie was crying and begging Moses to get someone to take them into town. So, that is what he did. All the way into town, Annie remained limp in her mother's arms. She did not appear to be breathing. But, as soon as they got into the doctor's office, into the light, Annie coughed and woke up. The doctor examined her and told her parents that she had whooping cough. The flashbacks, that Annie would later have throughout her childhood, were evidence of what likely was one of the youngest children having a "Near Death Experience", (NDE), known to man.

Annie had one of the residual side effects of NDE. She was moderately psychic. At the age of 12, she surprised her brothers and sisters that she knew that their uncle had died, before their father found out. They all wanted to know how she knew it. It was hard for Annie to explain her powers of discernment, that led her to this conclusion, before their dad went next door to answer the phone call from their Uncle Calvin in which he told Moses that his younger brother, Uncle Ben, had died. There were other occasions when Annie demonstrated pre-knowledge of certain events. Another possible reason that Annie was psychic, was that one day when they were all outside playing, Annie fell and hit her head on a rock. She lost consciousness and was out for approximately one-half hour while Maggie carried her up and down the stairs trying to wake her up. People who have such injuries do sometimes go on to display some psychic abilities.

CHAPTER SEVENTEEN

When Annie was eleven and Dorothy was ten someone gave the McCall family a used piano. Maggie, somehow, put aside one dollar per week so that they could take piano lessons from Mrs. Vernon, the organist at their church. Annie loved going to her house every week for lessons and she practiced diligently during the week. She could soon play simple hymns for Sunday school. Dorothy, on the other hand, did not like playing the piano. One day, when she was supposed to be practicing, Maggie heard loud banging coming from the living room where the piano was. When she went to the living room door and looked in, she saw Dorothy lying down on the piano bench, with her feet on the piano banging away. Needless to say, Dorothy did not take any more lessons.

Despite the above incident, Dorothy and Annie were very close. When they were younger, Maggie dressed them alike and they were almost like twins. When they became teenagers, and bought their own clothes, they still dressed alike at times. When Annie turned sixteen, Maggie allowed her to socialize a little more. After Church on Sunday evenings Annie and Dorothy were allowed to go to the Junior Elks Club to dance and socialize with the kids there. When prom time came they went, even though they did not have steady boyfriends. There was no money for expensive prom dresses, so they went to the Salvation Army thrift shop and bought used gowns, which Maggie altered. One day, about that time, Annie overheard one of the girls call her " Raggedy Ann." Such a slight did not even phase her that much because she knew that she would not always have to buy clothes from thrift shops. After all, she knew that when she graduated from high school, she was going to nursing school and, after that, she would have all the money she needed.

CHAPTER EIGHTEEN

Mount Union is a small town nestled in a valley surrounded by the Appalachian Mountains. It is located in central Pennsylvania approximately 35 miles from State College where Pennsylvania State University is located. In its heyday, it was a town of five to six thousand people. Much of the employment was in the three brick manufacturing plants where bricks were made out of the silica sand present in the area. The bricks were used in the steel mills in cities not far from there.

There was one high school, one junior high school, and one elementary school. Children came from outlying area farms and villages, near Mt. Union, to the high school and junior high school. There were elementary schools in the villages. When Annie went to high school, it was known as Captain Jack Joint High School. Captain Jack, as folk lore went, was a settler in the area who, on returning from a hunting trip, found his wife and children murdered by Native Americans. Now, the town is approximately one quarter African American and three quarters white. There are three African American churches and a great number of white churches. There was not much mixing of the two racial groups when Annie lived there.

CHAPTER NINETEEN

James Arthur was born on July 20, 1948. When they were preparing for his birth, Moses and Maggie decided to send their two oldest children, Annie and Dorothy, and their two youngest children, Ben and Jan, to Claysburg Pennsylvania, to let Moses' two brothers and their wives care for them. Annie and Dorothy were delighted. They were going to spend two whole weeks with their favorite cousin, Betty Mae. They loved their uncles and aunts also. They had a great time. They got a break from watching their younger siblings since a different aunt and uncle kept them. Annie celebrated her eleventh birthday while in Claysburg. Their Aunt Ethel had a surprise birthday party for her. It was the only birthday party that she had ever had. There wasn't time or money for parties in the Moses McCall family. Despite the good times, Dorothy and Annie were happy to get back home to see their new brother and to see John and Helaine, who had remained in Mt. Union and kept by Moses' cousin, Riley. While the four kids were in Claysburg, Moses had broken his leg while attending a baseball game. When Annie saw the cast on his leg, she burst into tears. She was not used to seeing her father injured.

Three and one-half years later, on December 26th, Gerald Eugene was born. By this time, Annie and Dorothy were fourteen and thirteen respectively and were old enough to watch the younger kids. Maggie had not been able to do much cooking. When Annie and Dorothy went to see her in the hospital, they surprised her by telling her that they had prepared a full turkey dinner by themselves. They had also washed all of the clothes. When Maggie got home the house was spotless. Her girls were really growing up! She was proud of them. Jerry was the eighth and final child that Moses and Maggie would have, as Maggie's doctor advised her against having any more children. That was alright with Moses and Maggie, as they felt their family was complete.

CHAPTER TWENTY

When Annie was fourteen years old, she and Dorothy, who shared a class, went to the principals' office to check out the ads for jobs there. They found housecleaning job offers and they followed in their Mother's footsteps and began cleaning white people's homes in the upper part of town. They would do these jobs after school, come home, do their chores, and then after supper, do their homework. They were both taking college preparatory classes and many times did not get to bed before midnight. Dorothy had decided that she, too, wanted to become a registered nurse. They did not know it at the time, but their two younger sisters, Helaine and Jan would adopt their dream and follow them into nursing schools.

Annie graduated from high school first. Since there was no money for her to go right into nursing school, she decided to work for a year first. She had had the foresight to take typing and stenography as electives in high school, so she applied for and obtained a job as a stenographer at the state capital in Harrisburg, Pennsylvania. In order to take this job, Annie had to go to Harrisburg to live. Maggie arranged for Annie to stay at the same boarding house as one of the girls from a well-respected family from church. The summer before her last year in high school, Annie had spent the summer staying with another family, who formerly lived in Mt. Union, who had moved to Lancaster, Pennsylvania. She worked cleaning houses there. This experience helped to prevent her from being homesick when she moved to Harrisburg. Also, Harrisburg was only two hours away and there was always someone making the trip to Mt. Union, with whom Annie could get a ride. Toward the end of that year, Annie took and passed the test required to enroll in Altoona Hospital School of Nursing in Altoona Pennsylvania. Dorothy, before graduating, had applied to and been accepted by Lewistown Hospital School of Nursing in Lewistown Pennsylvania. The two sisters entered their respective programs on the same day. Maggie went with Annie. Moses went with Dorothy. Both girls were very excited. Their dreams to become nurses were on the way to becoming true. They both received $350.00 loans to finance the three years it took to pay for their education. Their parents were also excited. Moses had only gone as far as the third grade, before he had to quit school to help his father on the sharecropper farm. Maggie had gone as far as tenth grade. Now their daughters, having graduated from high school, were on their way to higher education. Moses and Maggie were both very proud of their girls. They saw their daughters as setting fine examples for their six younger children. John was set to graduate the next year. Moses' and Maggie's education had had to be limited; they were happy to see their children accomplishing what they had been unable to do.

CHAPTER TWENTY-ONE

Although Annie and Dorothy chose to go to different nursing schools, their programs were much the same. Both of their programs began with a three month period, where they learned the scientific basis for nursing. They both received instruction in anatomy, physiology, chemistry, and biology. As a matter of fact, they had the same professors. The courses were taught by professors at branches of Pennsylvania State University. They taught Annie's classes on Mondays and Tuesdays and Dorothy's classes on Wednesdays and Thursdays. Since neither Annie nor Dorothy had classes on weekends, they were able to come home each weekend. At home, they compared experiences and grew closer as a result of having the same courses. They even studied together at home. As summer ended, they both were introduced to the practical side of nursing, learning the basis for nursing by means of classes and practical experience in their respective hospitals, Annie at Altoona General Hospital and Dorothy at Lewistown Hospital. They learned the fundamentals of nursing and soon were involved in patient care. At the beginning of their second year they were both put in charge of patient units.

At the beginning of their third year of nursing school, Annie and Dorothy decided to enter the Army Student Nurse Program. In this program, they were enlisted in the Army as privates and were paid as such. For this one year of being paid, they were required to enter the Army Nurse Corps as officers and were obligated to serve in this Corps for at least two years in return for the Army paying them for their last year of nursing school. When they told their parents of their intentions, Maggie was very upset. She voiced her concern that they would only be used by men in the Army. Annie and Dorothy tried to reassure their mother that they would be nurses the same as they would have been as civilians. Maggie continued to have reservations, however.

One night toward the end of Annie's third year of nursing school, she and a friend, Shirley, went for a walk downtown. On the way home, they were stopped by two of Shirley's friends in their car. Although Annie and Shirley were almost back at their residence, they decided to take Shirley's friend up on his offer to give them a ride. They got into the car with these friends and they all decided to drive to the Horseshoe Curve, a scenic part of the railroad in Altoona. While parked there, the car ran out of gas. Shirley and Annie became alarmed because they had a midnight curfew. Annie wanted to go to a house, where they could see lights in the distance. The other three people in the car wanted to wait until morning. That was what they did. Meanwhile back at the residence, the house-mother became alarmed when they did not return at midnight. She called the head of the program, Mrs. Smith. After waiting all night, Mrs. Smith called Annie and Shirley's parents to tell them that Annie and Shirley were missing.

After getting gas, by going to the same house where Annie wanted to go the night before, and calling roadside assistance, Shirley's friends took them back to their residence at 5AM. Mrs. Smith was waiting for them and let them know that they were in trouble. She told Annie and Shirley to call their parents to let them know that they were safe. This they did. Mrs. Smith then told them that they were suspended for one month and that they were to go home right away.

Annie's parents were glad that she was safe but they were disturbed that she had let herself get in so much trouble at the end of her education at the nursing school. Annie and Shirley graduated with their class, however. Then they had to make up the month for which the had been suspended.

During the time that all of the above was happening, during a routine physical, it was discovered that Annie had an enlarged lymph node in her neck and needed to have surgery. Annie was afraid it was malignant. She was relieved, when on meeting with the physician and Mrs. Smith, to find out that she had tuberculosis. This meant that she could not go right into the Army Nurse Corps, but that she had to have 18 months of treatment. Since Annie was still a member of the Armed Forces, the treatment would have to be in an Army Hospital. The closest one to Mt. Union was Valley Forge Army Hospital (VFAH) in Phoenixville, Pennsylvania. So instead of accompanying Dorothy to Harrisburg Pennsylvania to take the state board examination to become a registered nurse, Annie was sent to VFAH for treatment.

CHAPTER TWENTY-TWO

While at Valley Forge Army Hospital, Annie was in isolation for two weeks. Her tuberculosis was contained in her lymph nodes so there was no risk of infecting anyone. She was at first on a women's ward in the hospital's Isolation unit, but was soon moved to another ambulatory unit and permitted to go to the cafeteria for meals. This was the same cafeteria where all hospital employees and ambulatory patients ate. The unit that she was on, housed thirty other patients. Some of them were ill Army personnel like Annie. Others were dependents (mostly wives) of Army personnel. Annie quickly made friends with the other women and always had someone to walk to the cafeteria with. Her biggest problem was keeping busy. She and the other women played card games, checkers, and chess, but Annie was not used to having so much free time. She quickly found the hospital library and spent a lot of time reading. As she had not as yet taken her state board examinations required to become a registered nurse, Annie spent some of her time studying for the examination. She had had the foresight to bring some of her nursing books with her to the hospital.

Annie was treated with two anti-tuberculosis drugs. Soon after coming to the hospital, Annie learned that she had the choice of getting out of the Army for five years and re-enlisting at the end of the five years. She decided to stay in the Army and soon learned that her time at the hospital would be six months and then she could be transferred to Fort Sam Houston, Texas, where she would be commissioned as an officer, a second lieutenant. Dorothy was in Texas already and had written, telling Annie all about it. She was involved in nine weeks of basic orientation, learning how to become an officer in the Army Nurse Corps. Annie had all that to look forward to. For the first time in Annie's life her younger sister, Dorothy, was having an experience before she, the older sister, had it. Annie realized then how much competition there was between the two. Dorothy must have felt this competition all of her life.

Ironically, Dorothy chose to come to Valley Forge Army Hospital for her permanent assignment. She would be coming there around the same time that Annie was leaving to go to Texas. Dorothy had made many friends at Fort Sam Houston and gave Annie all of their names so Annie could look them up. Annie was looking forward to meeting her sister's friends, and knowing about them, increased Annie's eagerness to start her Army career. After taking and passing the state board examination, Annie was off to Texas.

CHAPTER TWENTY-THREE

Texas was all Dorothy promised and more. Here, Annie met people from all over the country. She met the friends of Dorothy and made friends of her own. Shortly after arriving there Annie was commissioned an officer in the Army Nurse Corps. The class was a large one of mostly female nurses, who had also joined the Army Student Nurse Program during their last year of nursing school just as Annie and Dorothy had done.

Annie chose to travel by train from Mt. Union to San Antonio, Texas. She arrived a few days before the nine weeks of classes started. There were other nurses already there as well. One day, Annie and two white nurses decided to go into town to the rodeo. After leaving the rodeo, they decided to go to a restaurant; it was a cafeteria styled one. As Annie and her two friends went through the line, selecting their food, Annie noticed several African American employees from the kitchen peering through the kitchen door at her. She thought nothing of it and approached the cashier. As she got there, the manager approached her. He said to Annie, "It is not our custom to serve Blacks in this restaurant." Now, Annie understood why the employees from the kitchen had been looking through the door at her. Annie felt indignation and embarrassment. This was what it felt like to live in the South in the 1960's. Annie and her two friends left their trays of food on the counter and left. They went around the corner to a five and ten cent store where they ordered food and ate standing up.

LESSONS IN LOVING

As classes began, the story of the incident spread throughout the class. Annie thought that everyone should have been as indignant as she was. This was not the case, however. Word got back to Annie that her commanding officer placed the blame squarely on Annie's shoulders. She supposedly said, "She should have known better. Her sister was just down here." when Annie received word of her commanding officer's reaction, she felt worse and more indignant. She thought the commanding officer should have been on her side. The Army used the Army Student Nurse Program to attract more nurses and this was how they were treated. The whole episode caused Annie to have negative feelings toward the Army.

Despite the above incident Annie enjoyed the time spent in Texas. She made new friends. She enjoyed meeting with them in the evenings at the Officers' Club. One Sunday afternoon a group of them went over the border into Mexico to attend a bullfight. This and other outings went a long way to erasing some of the negative feelings Annie felt toward the army.

One thing happened, however, that brought back some of the negative feelings: toward the end of the nine-week orientation, the group was tested to ascertain how they would perform as Army officers. When the tests had been graded, each student went to the Commanding Officer's office to get his or her grade. Annie happened to enter the office with one of the white male students. The Commanding Officer greeted them and said, "Oh, the top two students come together. "Congratulations, you got the highest grades!" The white male student got his grade and left. Only then did the Commanding Officer tell Annie that she had really got the highest grade but that she didn't want to hurt the male student's feelings. Annie felt that the officer should have been honest. She felt this especially when later she learned that the top student in the previous class had received special honors and commendations from the commanding general.

There were other health professionals learning how to be officers at Fort Sam Houston like the nurses. One such person was Sam Smith, a pharmacist. Annie met Sam during their second week there. She and Sam dated pretty often the rest of the time. They promised to keep in touch after they were permanently assigned.

LESSONS IN LOVING

Annie was going to be stationed at Valley Forge Army Hospital while Sam was going to a small post in upstate New York. It was while dating Sam that Annie decided to maintain her status as a virgin. She did this for two reasons. One, she was a devout Christian and two, she did not want to become pregnant. Her and Sam's relationship did not reach the point where it was a problem.

While at Fort Sam Houston, Annie corresponded with two patients she met when she was a patient at Valley Forge Army Hospital. One was Leon; the other was Samuel. Samuel was now stationed at Fort Dix, New Jersey. When Annie told Samuel that her sister Dorothy was now stationed at Valley Forge Army Hospital, Samuel put the wheels in motion to ensure that he and Annie would renew their relationship upon Annie's return to VFAH. He made arrangements to introduce Dorothy to a friend of his, a drill Sargent who was also stationed at Fort Dix. This friend was Broadus Mattison. When Samuel talked to Broadus about Dorothy, the first thing that Broadus said was, " If she is so nice, why don't you date her?" Samuel replied, "I am interested in her sister."

When Annie was given the chance to select her permanent assignment, she chose Fort Letterman in California as her first choice, VFAH as her second choice and a base in Virginia as her third choice. Annie had always wanted to go to California and thought it might be nice to spend her two years there. Then again, it would be good to be with her sister at VFAH. It was decided, by the powers that be, that Annie receive the second choice. She didn't mind that so much. Along with being with her sister, she was also content with this selection because she would be close to Mt. Union and could visit her family often. When it was determined that she and Dorothy were going to be together, they decided to buy a car together. Annie sent the money to Dorothy and Dorothy and Moses shopped for and bought a used Plymouth Horizon. So Annie had a lot to look forward to when she returned North.

CHAPTER TWENTY-FOUR

What an exciting time this was in Annie's life. It was a dream come true; a dream which started when Annie was nine years old and in fourth grade when her mother came home from the hospital after birthing Janelle, Annie's youngest sister. It was almost a year since Annie graduated from nursing school. Now, she was starting her career as a registered nurse. Actually, the work was easier than when Annie was in nursing school, in charge of a patient unit of very sick patients. The patients she had now were mostly ambulatory and not very sick. Annie's duties consisted of passing out medications, charting and supervising the corpsmen, who actually did most of the patient care. The unit Annie was on had forty male patients with a variety of medical and surgical diagnoses. Some were in traction for broken bones. Some had medical diagnoses such as early stage lung cancer or digestive disorders.

Annie was glad to be stationed with her sister, Dorothy. Dorothy worked on a women's ward down the hall from Annie's unit They often had the same days off. On those days, they got in their car and drove the Pennsylvania Turnpike to Mt. Union. It was about a four hour drive. They both became licensed drivers and, at times, they would work the evening shift, get off work, change clothes, and drive the four hours home. Moses and Maggie were always glad to see them, as were their younger siblings.

Annie and Dorothy had exciting social lives. The guys they were dating were good friends and they frequently double-dated. One evening Dorothy's friend Broadus and Samuel Duval, Annie's friend, decided to take Annie and Dorothy to New York City. There, they went to a night club, watched the floor show, and then went to a restaurant. On the way home they ran out of gas on the New Jersey Turnpike. While they were stopped, a couple stopped to ask them if they were going in the right direction for New York. Samuel told them that they were. He got a ride with them to get gas and, then, told them that they needed to turn around as they were not going in the right direction to New York. This subterfuge on Samuel's part caused the couple to be going back in the direction of the disabled car; thus Samuel got a ride back there.

Dorothy and Matt were really getting serious about each other and started talking of marriage. Matt bought Dorothy a lovely ring. Shortly there after, Samuel bought Annie a ring as well, although Annie was not quite sure that she was ready for marriage. She wore the ring, however.

As the summer wore on, Matt and Dorothy began looking for states in which they could be married. Dorothy told Maggie that she wanted to get married. Maggie was not in favor of that at all. Thus one evening after Matt and Dorothy got their license, Annie and Samuel went to the chapel with them and they got married. After socializing for a couple of hours at the Noncommissioned Officers Club, Annie and Dorothy returned to VFAH. The following weekend, Matt came to VFAH and then, he and Dorothy went to a local motel where they consummated their marriage.

Shortly after Dorothy and Matt got married, Annie gave Samuel his ring back. Whenever Samuel came to VFAH, he and Annie spent the evening together. Then Samuel would take her home. Annie knew that Samuel remained at VFAH overnight, but did not know what he did or with whom he did it. There was gossip about him, however. After hearing some of it, Annie decided that she no longer wanted to remain in the relationship.

CHAPTER TWENTY-FIVE

All service people are required to keep their immunizations up to date because of the possibility of suddenly being sent to serve in another part of the world. Thus it was that, one day after receiving a required diphtheria shot, Annie awakened feeling feverish and dizzy. Upon going to the dispensary, it was found that she had a fever of 103*F degrees. Since sick persons were not allowed to remain in their quarters, Annie was hospitalized. Since she continued with a fever, and had pain in the kidney area, other diagnostic tests were done. An intravenous pyelogram was done after Annie was referred to a urologist. He diagnosed her as having acute pyelonephritis and ordered her to be put on antibiotics. Annie's treatment for tubercular adenitis also continued. After two weeks in the hospital, Annie was discharged and was allowed to return to work. She was admonished to continue under the care of the urologist, however, since further testing showed that she had some kidney damage. Upon reading about her condition, Annie found that pyelonephritis was a chronic illness which could possibly shorten one's life span. She refused to dwell on it, however, and continued working and living her life, as before receiving the diagnosis.

As the summer turned to fall, Annie found herself easily fatigued and continued having pain in her upper back. Since she did not get better she was again hospitalized.

CHAPTER TWENTY-SIX

Because of Annie's frequent illnesses, her usually outgoing, positive attitude changed to one beset with withdrawal and depression. Even when one Sunday, before she was again hospitalized, her friend Sam, the pharmacist, came to visit her from New York. Their visit was a short one, as Sam could only stay one day, plus Annie had to work the evening shift on the day he visited. The visit was uneventful and Annie felt that she would not see him again. Two days after Sam's visit, Annie was admitted to the hospital after she visited the dispensary complaining of upper back pain and fatigue. Once in the hospital Annie was subjected to test after test. Some of the tests showed that her pyelonephritis continued. Also, she was still being treated for tuberculosis. Her physician was a young captain from New England. He ordered consultations with physicians in other disciplines. Some of the tests caused the doctors to consider Addison's disease. This diagnosis was not conclusive, however; the hunt for the cause of Annie's back pain, depression, and fatigue continued. She was even sent to the Naval Hospital in Philadelphia for tests. Her attending physician, Dr. Haley came into her room every morning with results of tests done the previous day. At times, he sat and talked with Annie. One day he bought a book that he had told Annie about which he said would help her deal with her illnesses. Some times he told Annie about experiences he had the previous weekend. Their patient/doctor relationship was a close one. Annie looked forward to his daily visits.

Finally after being in the hospital for two months and with most of the tests being negative, Annie was referred to a psychiatrist. She was not surprised as this was the usual course, when very little physical evidence was forth coming. After meeting with him several times, he recommended that Annie be discharged and to continue seeing a psychiatrist as an out patient.

After her discharge, Annie visited the psychiatrist one time. At this meeting he asked her, "Were you always alone when you were growing up?" Annie looked at the psychiatrist curiously and asked, "How can you be alone with nine other people in the house?" With that, the psychiatrist said, "Well, if you feel that you need me, make an appointment." That was the end of Annie's psychiatric treatment.

Annie missed the long talks and attention paid to her by Dr. Haley. They dated a few times but discontinued dating because, according to Dr. Haley, "The base is too small for a relationship like ours." He was white and she was African American. Annie had no choice but to accept his conclusion.

Dorothy was supportive during Annie's illness. As a matter of fact, Annie was hospitalized in Dorothy's unit and she was often Annie's nurse. But Dorothy had her own problems. Her husband, Matt, had gone to Korea in September and she missed him badly. She lived for his daily letters and regaled Annie daily with some of their contents. Annie tried to be a good listener and their close relationship continued.

Annie was now working on the pediatric ward, caring for the children of Army personnel. She loved her work; it was rewarding and she felt that she really helped the children, her life- long reason for wanting to become a nurse.

Annie's time in the Army Nurse Corps was winding down. When the Berlin wall went up, everybody's time in the service was extended for one year. When the war stayed cold, the extension was shortened to six months. Annie was glad for her Army career to be over. The fact that she and Dorothy had been unable to get time off to go to their grandfather's funeral confirmed their decision not to re-enlist. They had given back the time required (plus six months) for the year that they had been paid while still in school. Now it was time to see how nursing as civilians would be.

Matt returned from Korea; he was stationed in Georgia. Dorothy transferred there for her last months in the Army and, now she was pregnant. Annie wanted to go back to school to earn her Bachelor in nursing degree.

CHAPTER TWENTY-SEVEN

While working on the pediatric floor Annie began noticing a nagging pain in her lower back. She had been lifting heavy kids into their cribs and tugging on the rusty side rails, which contributed to the pain.

Annie spent her last shift in the Army working with sick children. Although six of them had fevers when Annie reported for duty, by the time the day nurses came on duty, every one of the feverish children had normal temperatures, mainly because of the hard work which Annie and her aide did, sponging and bathing them. At the end of the shift, Annie was worn out and experiencing severe pain in her lower back. She went straight to see the orthopedic doctor, who admitted her to the hospital and ordered her to be put in the William's position (head and knees elevated). Thus, Annie spent her last three weeks in the Army on bedrest and in this position. She was discharged from the hospital and when she mustered out of the Army, the Sargent took care to mention that she had a back injury sustained while she working in the Army.

CHAPTER TWENTY-EIGHT

After spending a restful summer with her parents and younger siblings, Annie moved to Philadelphia. She wanted to find a job and to make arrangements to attend the University of Pennsylvania. This school was the only one in the country to offer a Bachelor of Science degree in Nursing. Right away Annie found a job as a staff nurse at the Veteran's hospital. The work was much harder there than that in the Army. For example, she and an aide were responsible for forty patients on the evening and night shifts. Twenty of them were very sick. Annie was sick frequently with kidney infections, missing work. At the end of the year Annie was pleasantly surprised to find out that the Veteran Administration wanted to pay for her to attend the University of Pennsylvania. They said that, rather than be a staff nurse, it would be better and easier for her to be a nursing instructor. They would not only pay her tuition, but would also pay her a small stipend. Thus, rather than attend school part time as she planned to do, Annie could now attend full time. The counselor at the VA arranged for Annie to begin school immediately. This she did. Because of the stipend, Annie would only have to do private duty nursing on a part-time basis. Since she shared an apartment with her sister, Helaine, her expenses were not too great. Helaine graduated from the same school of nursing as Dorothy had, a few months earlier. She was working at the Hospital of the University of Pennsylvania as a staff nurse and would soon take her state board examinations.

LESSONS IN LOVING

Life was good for both sisters as they adjusted to living in Philadelphia. Annie enjoyed going to classes at Penn. She met many people, whom she never would have met if she hadn't been in school. For example, there were many African students, especially from Nigeria, Kenya, and Ghana. These countries were newly independent and sent many of their residents to schools in the West. Annie met Lawrence in her first class. He was a Nigerian pre-med student and he and Annie started dating right away. He sought her out during the break in classes on the first day of their Philosophy class. Lawrence wanted to become a doctor and then return to his country to provide badly needed medical care to his people. Since Annie became a nurse in order to help people, she and Lawrence had much in common. They also had many conversations about the racial problems in America and the lack thereof in Nigeria's new found independence from Great Britain. Annie never would have met someone like Lawrence if she had stayed in Mt. Union. As they got closer, Lawrence wanted more from Annie than she was willing to give. She was still a virgin and did not think that Lawrence was someone with whom she had a future since he planned to return to Nigeria. This did not jive with Annie's plans. They soon became just platonic friends, seeing each other only at parties. Each had moved on.

Annie's brother, Ben, who had graduated from high school and moved to Philadelphia, introduced Annie to Paul. Paul was a high school English teacher. He attended Annie's church. Paul and Annie became very good friends. He hailed from a small town in the Midwest, He had that in common with Annie. Their relationship blossomed, and they would have become even closer, except for something that happened one evening when Paul came to visit Annie. Paul forced himself on Annie and engaged in what would be termed date rape if it happened today. As it was, Annie felt that she had been robbed, but she continued to see Paul. The experience had not been a good one. The event concluded by Paul telling Annie, "Go wash yourself so you won't become pregnant," treating it as though it was a shameful experience, which needed to be "washed away." This episode marked a turning point in Annie's and Paul's relationship. They continued dating but things were different. They were still close, however Annie thought Paul was going to propose, but he didn't. Christmas was approaching and Annie expected a ring. However, Paul let her know that he was going to Indiana for the holidays, and that he would bring her Christmas gift back with him. Annie went to Mt. Union for the holidays. A lot of the time when everyone else was talking and laughing downstairs, Annie was upstairs in bed. Moses even asked her if she felt alright on one occasion. Annie assured him that she was ok. When she returned to Philadelphia, Paul gave her his Christmas gifts: A Bible and a pearl necklace. Annie hid her disappointment that no ring was forthcoming. As time went on, they drifted farther and farther apart, until gradually they stopped communicating at all. Annie heard from her brother that Paul was dating other people: She thought to herself, "Oh well another relationship bites the dust."

CHAPTER TWENTY-NINE

While Annie's love life left a lot to be desired, her nursing career was moving right along. She graduated from the University of Pennsylvania, and, right away, obtained a position as clinical instructor in their Hospital School of Nursing. Annie liked working there very much. Since she taught students in the clinical area, she still had very much contact with patients. While she performed no patient care herself, she supervised students as they carried out patient care and procedures. They were on a surgical unit, caring for patients both before and after surgery. This unit was a large one, having twenty patients in an open ward. The students, working under Annie, did dressing changes, catheter care, bathing patients, feeding patients and many other procedures that pre-operative and post-operative patients needed.

Annie had worked there for one year, when she was offered a job working in a dispensary in a large federal office building, caring for civilian employees, who, during their work day received such injuries as paper cuts, sprains, strains, and different medical diagnoses for which they needed help. Her duties also included pre-employment physical examinations which included blood and urine collection. Annie knew that eventually she wanted to teach on the college level and wanted to get experience in as many different kinds of nursing as possible. She knew that, in addition to her Bachelor of Science Degree in Nursing, she would also be required to have a Masters degree. While she was attending Penn, Annie did private duty nursing during school breaks. Now she was in an entirely different kind of nursing, which she thoroughly enjoyed. At the Signal Corp, where she worked, Annie had a chance to do much patient teaching to employees who came to the dispensary suffering from acute attacks of various chronic illnesses. This was very different from the other kinds of nursing which Annie had done.

Annie left the job in the dispensary after two years to go to school to get the aforementioned Master's degree. She obtained a grant, which included a small stipend for living expenses. Annie again enrolled at the University of Pennsylvania. After two week of school, Annie made an appointment to see the dean. She did this because her teachers were assigning the same articles and books which Annie had read as an undergraduate. When she met with the dean and discussed her dilemma, the dean told her that perhaps it would be better for Annie to obtain a Master's in Education degree rather than one in nursing, the field she was enrolled in. On the basis of the dean's suggestion, Annie withdrew from the Master's in Nursing program.

CHAPTER THIRTY

Though successful in her nursing career, Annie remained unmarried and childless. Her sisters were now all married. Helaine married a neighbor of theirs in their first apartment when they first moved to Philadelphia. They were married at a justice of the peace and had a party at her husband's sister's house that evening. Moses and Maggie were alerted and spent the weekend in Philadelphia. Helaine and Malcom, her new husband, lived a few blocks from Annie. Annie and Helaine's youngest sister, Janelle, did not attend Helaine's wedding party as she was now in Texas, having left nursing school a few months earlier in order to get married. Her husband was in the Army.

Dorothy and Matt lived in Baltimore. They had three children now, recently having had twins. Matt continued his career as a Sargent in the Army. He taught in the ROTC program at Morgan State University. Dorothy worked as a private duty nurse in a hospital in Baltimore on the night shift so that Matt could watch the children. They were both taking courses in Business Administration at Morgan.

While working at the Hospital of the University of Pennsylvania and later at the Signal Corps. Annie lived in the Penn area on the second floor of a three- story house converted into three apartments. The first floor was rented to a dentist and his family. A graduate student lived on the third floor. One day on returning home from work Annie found a note, written by the graduate student, telling her that all three of the apartments had been robbed. She found that the robber took a typewriter and some money from her. While Annie's loss was not great, she immediately began looking for a new apartment. Not long afterwards, Annie moved to a swanky high rise in center city Philadelphia on Benjamin Franklin Parkway. It was while living here that Annie decided to investigate computer dating. It was through this type of dating that she met Thad Carter, a Philadelphia policeman. They connected right away and soon agreed that they would limit dating to each other. One thing worried Annie about Thad however: He was a pretty heavy drinker. Nevertheless, they continued getting closer, and three months after meeting, they decided to get married. Thad was a widower, having lost his second wife three years earlier. Annie thought that this was probably why he drank so much. She thought that after they got married, he probably would not drink as much.

Thad and Annie decided to have a large wedding since it was her first marriage. They spent the next three months planning the wedding. Annie chose Dorothy as her maid of honor and Helaine and Janelle as her bridesmaids. She decided to get married in Mt. Union. Her whole family was involved in preparing for the wedding. It turned out to be a grand affair with people attending from all over the country. They had a sit- down dinner for one hundred fifty people. Annie and Thad spent a week in Jamaica on their honeymoon. Annie moved out of her high-rise apartment into Thad's house in the Germantown section of Philadelphia.

CHAPTER THIRTY-ONE

A few months before marrying, Annie got a new job inspecting nursing homes for state licensing and Medicare certification. She continued here after her marriage. She and Thad had decided not to use any birth control and to let "nature take its course", as Thad put it. Thad was assigned to a district not far from their home. He worked on rotating shifts and had two different days off each week. One day, about six weeks after they had been married, Annie came home from work and found Thad and three of his friends in the kitchen, playing cards. They had been drinking and apparently had been playing cards all day. Annie went into the kitchen and greeted Thad and his guests. When she attempted to make small talk, to show that they were welcome to their home, Thad got angry with her and told her to leave the kitchen. He said, "You're always trying to be the center of attention. Go upstairs." Annie was very hurt that Thad would talk that way to her, in front of quests. She left the kitchen and went upstairs. Shortly thereafter, she heard Thad and his guests leave. He did not tell her where he was going or even say "Goodbye".

Annie was still upset and remained upstairs, not even going downstairs to eat. Thad returned about three hours later. Annie pretended to be asleep but saw, through half closed eyes, that when Thad took his shirt off, there was lipstick on his undershirt. She was heartsick when she realized that he had been unfaithful.

The next day Annie got up and got dressed as though she was going to work. She did not go, however, but called in sick and went downtown to the movies. She was gone all day, trying to figure out what to do. She wanted to leave but in the end decided not to. She went home to face Thad and from then on, things went downhill. They went to a marriage counselor and things seemed to improve. Annie started experiencing a lot of back pain and was hospitalized for 10 days.

Two months went by, Annie had missed her period that month and, since she was always regular, she thought she might be pregnant. On the very last day of the year, Annie and Thad went to see her obstetrician, who confirmed that Annie was indeed, two months pregnant. She was concerned because when she was hospitalized, she had had back x-rays. Hopefully they would not affect the baby.

Annie was very sick during her first trimester. She was nauseated and vomited for most of the day and could only eat at night. This, along with her continuing back pain, caused her to have to leave her position with the state. Since, with the advent of her second trimester, she began to feel better. Annie decided to return to private duty nursing. Thad wrecked his car and had been using Annie's car. Since she was going back to work, she told Thad that she would need her car. Thad was upset and told Annie that he wanted the keys to his house. Consequently, when he went to work that day, he locked the dead bolt lock to the house, locking Annie in the house. They had not been getting along and this was the last straw. Thad stayed out late every night; sometimes, he did not return until morning. They were now sleeping in separate rooms. Annie decided to leave since the situation was rapidly deteriorating and Thad did not seem to care for her any longer.

Annie called her sister Helaine, and arranged to move in with her. She packed her belongings and called a moving company to help her move the furniture that she had kept from her apartment. She arranged with her brother, Ben, to store some of her furniture in his basement. When the movers came the next day, Thad was mostly silent, speaking only to the movers when one of the men accidently knocked a picture off the wall. There was no conversation between him and Annie.

Annie moved in with her sister who, at the time was divorcing her husband of four years. Helaine worked for Medicare at an insurance company in the suburbs. Annie and her sisters were always close and she and Helaine got along fine, often going out together. They went to Mt. Union one weekend to attend Jerry, her youngest brother's graduation from high school and Jim's graduation from college. Annie continued doing private duty nursing until her eighth month, and would have worked longer except that her patients were concerned about her. She went to Temple University one weekend to take the Graduate Records Examination, as she planned to begin working on her Master's degree after the baby was born.

CHAPTER THIRTY-TWO

Although pregnant and looking forward to the birth of her baby, Annie had bad feelings toward Thad. The summer of 1969, he wined and dined her and professed his love. At the end of the summer he made what should have been, lasting promises to her. Now, the summer of 1970, she was alone, while he was most likely, wining and dining someone else. Once, during that summer, when he asked for and received permission to take her out to lunch, they did not even make it to the restaurant when something he said, caused Annie to jump out of the car, only a few blocks from the house. When the baby, whom Annie named Anderson McCall Carter, was born, instead to calling Thad to tell him of the birth Annie called his mother. Thad came to the hospital the next day and also on the day she and the baby were discharged. He followed behind them as Annie and Anderson rode home with Helaine. Annie had prepared for Ander, as she called him, by buying a bassinet and clothing with the money her lawyer arranged for Thad to pay. When they got to Helaine's house, they spent an awkward half hour in the living room before Thad left.

Annie had saved enough money so that she would not have to work for six weeks. In the meantime, she and Helaine moved to a mid-rise apartment building in the suburbs. It was a large apartment: Annie had a large bedroom and bath, as did Helaine. There was a thirty-foot-long living room, kitchen, and a balcony. They each had separate telephone lines. Shortly after moving there, Annie started back working three nights a week while Helaine watched Ander. They lived there for almost a year, when Helaine decided to move to Baltimore to work at the Social Security Administration. After Helaine left, Annie and Ander moved to a smaller apartment in the same building. Before she moved, Annie and Thad had a reconciliation which lasted about four months. Thad was crazy about Ander and came by to get him whenever he had a chance.

CHAPTER THIRTY-THREE

When Ander was one year old, Annie enrolled at Temple University to begin work on her Master of Education degree. With the help of a small loan, coupled with the money she received from the Veteran's Administration, she was able to go to school full time. Her aim was to get the degree and then teach at the Community College of Philadelphia, (CCP). By doing this, she would have shorter working hours and thus be able to spend more time with her child. Her second reason for wanting to teach at this college was because she wanted to be an example to the students there, especially black women, who would be more likely to attend this type of institution. Just as Mrs. Singh, back in Pennsylvania, had let Annie know that she could become a nurse, Annie considered it her duty to inspire others to aim higher.

Mrs. Davis, an elderly lady living in the small town not far from Annie's apartment building, came three evenings a week to baby sit for Ander while Annie went to school. By attending night school, she was able to spend all day with Ander. She would leave the house at six-thirty PM, by which time it was Ander's bedtime. Thus, Mrs. Davis had only to sit there the three hours that Annie was gone. Annie hired Mrs. Davis through a child care agency, advertising in the local newspaper. Mrs. Davis was very reliable and she lived on a street through which the apartment bus went every hour. Thus, Annie did not have to pay for her transportation to the apartment, but only pay the three-dollar taxi fare for her to return home, by which time the apartment bus had stopped running. Since Mrs. Davis was so reliable, she was able to sit for Ander the whole three semesters Annie needed to complete the courses for her Master's degree. During the day, Annie would get Ander up, feed him breakfast, and then they would go to the playground for an hour or two. Then it was back home for lunch and a nap, during which time Annie could study. By six-thirty PM, when Ander was just about ready for bed, Annie kissed him goodnight and left him in Mrs. Davis' care. She then drove into the city for her classes, returning at ten-thirty PM to relieve Mrs. Davis. By the time Annie finished her course work, Ander was two and one-half years old. A few months earlier Annie had taken him to a nearby laboratory nursery school run by a junior college. Ander seemed to enjoy the hour he spent there; he readily joined in playing with the children and seemed genuinely disappointed when it was time to leave. Annie planned to enroll him in this nursery school when she returned to work. She had already applied for a job at CCP. Because of her education and work experience, she was easily accepted and began working there at the beginning of the Spring semester, 1973.

CHAPTER THIRTY-FOUR

When Ander was almost two, his parents reconciled again. Thad had spent three months in alcohol rehabilitation at Philadelphia General Hospital. After his discharge, he contacted Annie, and they began dating again. When they reconciled, Thad lived with Annie and Ander at their apartment in the suburbs. Annie refused to move back to Thad's house in the city. Although Thad had started divorce proceedings the year before, he contacted his lawyer and told him to withdraw it. Annie loved Thad, in spite of his womanizing, and agreed to try again. After all they did have a child together, who would benefit from a stable home. They had been back together for about four months when Thad started talking about killing Annie.

One day they were sitting on the sofa, talking, when Thad said, "I could have you killed and make it look like a suicide." This upset Annie. The way she understood it, was that Thad wanted the marriage to work, but he didn't know how to make it work. He was almost desperate. Annie wrote a letter to her brother, John telling him, that in case she ended up dead, Thad was the cause. She put the letter where John could find it in case of her death. A few weeks went by. One-day Thad said, "I could blow your brains out." Annie made up her mind then and there to end the marriage. She let Thad know. He agreed and told Annie to file for the divorce this time and that he would pay for it. Annie thought that divorcing was the right way to go. There was no point continuing and running the risk of Ander having one parent dead and the other in prison. She contacted her lawyer and started divorce proceedings. It took about eight months for it to finalize. They still had contact, as Thad continued keeping Ander on his days off. This arrangement would continue until Ander was eighteen years old. Their contacts were cordial and uneventful, however.

CHAPTER THIRTY-FIVE

Annie began teaching at the Community College of Philadelphia in January 1973. It was rewarding work. Two days a week, she taught students on patient floors in hospitals, as they cared for patients. Two days a week, she taught students in the classroom. They had what is known as "Team Teaching" in the Nursing Department. A team, consisted of usually seven professors, who took turns teaching, usually about fifty students, in either the first or second year of the Nursing Program. While one professor is lecturing, the other six professors are required to be in the classroom, also. That way, they were all aware of what information their students received. They each had groups of ten or less in their group. Annie usually taught students in the second year of the program. On Mondays, the professors had meetings, either team meetings and/or Department meetings. Each professor was required to be available to students five hours per week for counseling and advising. The total hours that Annie was required to be, either in the classroom, at the hospital, or in her office amounted to approximately thirty hours per week. These shorter hours made it possible for Annie to spend more time with Ander. He got on the nursery school bus each morning at eight-thirty cheerfully saying "Good morning" to Jack, the driver, and sitting down and waving "good-bye" to Annie. He returned on the bus at four in the afternoon. Annie hired a lady to meet the bus if she was going to be late returning from the college.

Ander loved attending nursery school and easily made friends. Sammy and Jonathon were two of his closest friends. He talked about them all the time. He learned a lot at the school and could count to twenty and could say all of his ABC's. He looked forward to each day and readily got on the bus each morning. Life was good for both Annie and Ander. They were glad to spend time together on weekends, however. Annie did not have to teach during the summer months; this let her spend time with Ander, helping him learn to swim among other things. He was now almost three and also had playmates at the apartment. Annie took him to the playground every day, where he played with other kids.

CHAPTER THIRTY-SIX

As Ander got older, the apartment seemed smaller and smaller as the years went by. Annie considered moving to a bigger apartment but thought of buying a house instead. Thus, she decided to enroll Ander in a day camp during the summer of 1974 and 1975. Since she was paid every two weeks year-round by the college, she decided to work elsewhere during the summer of those years, making extra money, and saving it to buy a house. So, when Ander was five and entering kindergarten, Annie bought a brand new four-bedroom house. Helaine came for the weekend from Baltimore caring for Ander, while Annie moved from the apartment to the house in Delaware County. When she signed the contract for the house, the builder came to see her, because he had some concerns because of Annie's race. Apparently, she was the only African American buying in the development. So, it happened that on the first night in the new house, Annie and Helaine joked about the possibility of someone throwing a brick thru the window. Nothing like that happened and the next day several of her neighbors in the development came over to welcome them to the neighborhood. Annie was the last one to move into the development. Her house had been the sample house and they had all been in the house.

All of Annie's brothers and sisters had graduated from high school and were living in the Baltimore/Washington area or in Philadelphia. They got together frequently over holidays and vacations for cookouts and the like. Since Annie now had the space, they all visited her frequently. She, likewise, went to their homes several times a year for outings in their area. Their children all knew each other well, Moses and Maggie visited their children often also. They were proud of their children, as all of them had gone on to get higher degrees. Several were teachers. And Jim was a lawyer with the Teamsters Union. John lived about fifteen minutes from Annie's house in the Philadelphia area and stopped by all the time. They were an extremely close family. The youngest brother, Jerry, had changed his name to Mamadou Chinyelu and worked as a journalist. He had written several books and numerous articles. Ben was an accountant. John managed a shoe store. Helaine and Janelle had both graduated from nursing school and had good jobs in the health care industry.

CHAPTER THIRTY-SEVEN

The summer of 1978, Annie chose to spend her summer as the school nurse at the Philadelphia College of Art. The regular nurse there, had school age children and wanted to be home with them in the summer. Annie's child, Ander, wanted to go to day camp that summer, freeing her to take the job.

Every day she drove to the train station, taking it into center city Philadelphia. She, then, walked the approximately fifteen blocks to the College of Art. By the end of the summer Annie was experiencing a considerable amount of pain in her low back area. Several years before, her gynecologist had told her that she had uterine fibroids and that she eventually would have to have surgery. She thought that the pain was caused by the fibroids and made an appointment with Dr. Smith, her gynecologist. He told her that the fibroids had indeed gotten larger and that she needed surgery. At the end of the summer, after arranging with her family to take care of Ander, Annie had a complete hysterectomy. Her sister, Dorothy, and her family, came to be with Annie on her surgery day. They, then, took Ander to Baltimore for two weeks. After Annie was discharged, her parents came to spend a week with her. As they prepared to leave, Helaine and her daughter, Melanie, brought Ander home. They spent a week with Annie, after which Annie's cousin, Sheila, came for a week. All in all, Annie was well taken care of and was grateful to her family for looking out for her.

CHAPTER THIRTY-EIGHT

Annie recuperated nicely from her abdominal surgery. One problem remained, however: she continued having pain in her low back area. Thinking that there was a problem with her kidneys, her physician ordered an intravenous pyelogram (IVP) after all her physical history showed that she had been diagnosed with pyelonephritis in her early twenties. The IVP was normal. This surprised Annie. She had been told back in the 60's that she had irreversible kidney damage. Apparently, healing had taken place. Since there was no problem with her kidneys, the gynecologist referred Annie to a neurologist, Dr. Edgar Kenton. Upon examination, Dr. Kenton noted that there was weakness in both her legs and some abnormal reflexes. Dr. Kenton ordered lumber traction at home, as Annie told him she did not want to be hospitalized. After six weeks of traction, Dr. Kenton told Annie that she possibly had a herniated disc in her low back and that she needed to be hospitalized for further tests and treatment. Reluctantly, Annie agreed to hospitalization and arranged for Moses and Maggie to come to stay with Ander.

In the hospital, Annie was tested extensively, and Dr. Kenton told Annie his findings: He said he thought that Annie had Multiple Sclerosis (MS). He said that, in light of her physical history, she had first shown signs of it back in 1960, when doctors in the Army hospital had been unable to diagnose her and had referred her to a psychiatrist. He said he had found weakness in both legs and in her right arm. He had also found nystagmus in her eyes. Dr. Kenton wrote prescriptions for large doses of prednisone every other day, as well as muscle relaxants and pain medication. According to Dr. Kenton, Annie's return to work was uncertain.

Annie was greatly disturbed when Dr. Kenton told her of his findings. She was not too familiar with the diagnosis of Multiple Sclerosis. Therefore, the next day, when she was discharged and her parents asked her what the doctor said was wrong with her, she told them that he said she had arthritis. She wanted to research the diagnosis in her medical-surgical text book and try to deal with it herself, before talking to her parents about it.

CHAPTER THIRTY-NINE

When Ander started school, Annie enrolled him in a Catholic school not far from where they lived. There was a Montessori pre-school in the basement of the school building. Since his Kindergarten was only half day, his Kindergarten teacher would walk him and other day care students' downstairs to the pre-school. At the end of her work day, Annie would pick Ander up there. Since her work day was longer than his school day when he was in first and second grades, Ander continued going to the Montessori School. When he reached third grade, Annie decided to enroll Ander in public school down the street from their house. She did this for two reasons: One was because she and Ander now regularly attended Zion Baptist Church in Ardmore, and she did not want him to be confused as far as the differences between what was taught in Catholic school and what he learned at the Baptist church. Second, she was not able to work, so there was no need for childcare after the school day was over.

Annie thought it important to expose Ander to teaching in a formalized religious setting. Her parents had seen fit to expose her and her brothers and sisters to such an experience. She knew what a comfort it was to her now. She wanted Ander to have the same benefit. The way the world was, a child needed all the help available to him or her with which to face life. Additionally, church was another place where he could meet children with similar back grounds.

When Ander completed third grade and came home ready for summer to begin, he was excited about a reading program which his teacher told him about. He was to read a certain number of books in honor of Multiple Sclerosis. The teacher showed them a movie about Multiple Sclerosis. Annie mistakenly took this opportunity to tell Ander that she had Multiple Sclerosis. Ander became very upset. Apparently, the movie depicted people with severe types of MS, some of whom were in wheelchairs. Even though Annie tried to convince Ander that she would not end up in a wheelchair, he refused to participate in the reading program. Annie felt bad about that and, too late, realized that she should have first determined what was in the film they had seen before telling Ander that she had MS.

CHAPTER FORTY

In 1975, shortly after moving to their new house, Annie decided to start working on her Doctoral degree. She had now worked at CCP for two years, and she knew that if she would want to teach in a four-year nursing program, she would need it. Therefore, she enrolled at Temple University and began work toward a Doctorate of Education degree.

That year Annie taught pediatrics. There was a need for a pediatric professor to supervise and teach students on the afternoon shift at Children's Hospital of Philadelphia (CHOP). Annie went to classes in the morning at Temple University and volunteered to work the afternoon shift with students at CHOP. This worked out very well, but it made for a long day for Annie. She would take Ander to school, go to Temple for classes and then leave there to go to CHOP. She ate lunch on the way while in the car. At CHOP, she taught from 2pm until 8pm. She would go home just in time to read to Ander before putting him to bed. She arranged for a sitter from the childcare agency to pick him up from school. This lady also prepared his evening meal and helped him with his bath. Those days were indeed long, but they only occurred two days a week and for only one semester.

When Annie got sick in 1978, she had completed all the course work for her Doctoral degree. She had only to complete her doctoral dissertation, and she had done the practical work for it. The rest of the work could be done at home and in the library. Annie had to meet with her advisors once a month and had to register for one course per semester. Since she was on disability and on pain medication, Annie took public transportation into the city once a month. When Annie sent her bill for the reimbursement for half her tuition from CCP, her department head balked at paying it, but relented when Annie told him that work on her dissertation was like occupational therapy for her. Annie also volunteered to be den mother for her son's Cub Scout troop.

During her disability, Annie also continued taking Ander to church each Sunday. When the people at Sunday School learned that she was a teacher, they asked her to teach a class there. This she did; since she had previously taught Sunday school when she was a teenager, this was not a problem.

Thad picked Ander up and spent weekends with him at least once a month. When Ander left, Annie was glad to have some time to herself. This happened on Friday. By Sunday evening when it was time for Thad to bring Ander back, Annie was missing Ander something terribly and was glad when he returned. The Monday following his visit, Ander was always hyperactive and his teacher would complain to Annie that he acted out in class. This was to become more of a problem as he got older. Annie suspected that while he was with Thad he had eaten much junk food such as sodas and candy. Annie made a note to speak to Thad about what Ander ate while he and Ander were together. She had already talked to Thad about the necessity to avoid letting anyone kiss Ander with lipstick on, as once he developed a running sore on his face after such an occurrence. He was allergic to lipstick.

CHAPTER FORTY-ONE

For every degree that Annie got, her sister, Dorothy, got one as well. Although Dorothy had four children, she worked, doing private duty nursing, while going to Morgan State University with her husband, Matt, where they each received Bachelor degrees in Business Administration; so, she went on to get a Master's degree in that discipline. Around the time that Annie began working on her dissertation, Dorothy began taking the train into Washington, DC three evenings a week, starting work on her Doctoral degree at George Washington University. After receiving her Master's degree; she had begun teaching Business Administration at Morgan State University. Although she and Annie did not live near each other, they remained close and took similar career paths.

    Annie finished work on her dissertation and successfully defended it to the satisfaction of her three advisors and graduated from Temple University in May 1980. The weekend before she graduated, two of her sisters, Helaine and Janelle, and their families came to help Annie celebrate. Later in the week Moses and Maggie drove down so they could attend the actual ceremony. John and his son, Rod, attended, as did Ander. Lynne, John's wife, took the day off work in order to prepare a lunch for everybody. It was a big day for the McCall family. They now had a doctor in the family. Their other big day was when Jim graduated from Catholic University with a Law degree. Not bad for two parents who did not even have a high school diploma. They had always let their children know how important education was to their future and they were very proud of them.

Annie had wanted to return to work in 1980 but her doctor prescribed certain limitations: no prolonged standing or walking. The college said that Annie could only come back if she was able to do everything the job entailed. She waited a few months and then decided to take a job part-time, calling pediatricians, encouraging them to buy measles, mumps, and rubella vaccines. She did well and thus, decided to try to get her regular job back. Annie's department head said she could use a wheelchair. However, Annie's doctor refused to write a prescription for one, as he said she didn't need a wheelchair. He told her to have her brother, the lawyer, fight for the kind of job she needed. In the end, Annie decided to go back to working at CCP without a wheelchair. She would sit when she could, teaching students that way.

In 1981, after marrying William Freeman, a deacon at Annie's church, Annie started back to work. She was able to supervise students in patient rooms, at times, standing. Other times, while counseling students and reviewing their notes in patient's charts, she would sit. At first, the hospital personnel where Annie taught students, thought she sat too much. The Director of Nursing wrote a letter to Annie's Department Head, saying this. The College considered putting her back on sick leave, this time without pay. Annie contacted Jim, her lawyer. He was now working at the National Labor Relations Board and was very knowledgeable as to what employers could and could not do. He wrote to the college lawyers, telling them that they could not put her back on leave based on anything stated in the Director of Nursing's letter. The Department Head then assigned Annie to a different hospital where the personnel understood that she would be sitting at times while teaching and counseling students. Other times, she would stand. Things worked out well at the new hospital. Annie was able to carry out her teaching without short changing students.

She continued to suffer some pain in her back. At the beginning of each semester, she was fine. As the semester went on the pain got progressively worse. By the end of the semester, Annie was looking forward to the semester break, when she could recuperate. Thus, she was able to work for six more years until one day she knew she could no longer. That morning, Annie called her Department Head and told her that she could not continue. After that Annie sat down and had a long cry. She knew that she had come to the end of the line, and that she would never work again. She had done everything possible to remain an active member of the working class. She even had gotten another degree, a Masters in Nursing, when the State Board of Nursing passed a regulation stating that if you were teaching nursing, you had to have a Master's degree in Nursing. The college had not really wanted her to return from disability leave, and there were rumors that professors were going to be declared incompetent if they did not get this degree. After Annie took the ten courses required for the degree at Villanova University, the rumors stopped. At any rate, Annie had done all she could to remain a member of the working class. At least she worked until she was almost fifty.

CHAPTER FORTY-TWO

Ander was an usher in the Junior Usher Board at church. The adult sponsor was Deacon Willie Freeman. Frequently, Deacon Freeman found it necessary to seek Annie out to tell her the type of clothing Ander needed to wear on the Sunday which he ushered on. One day, Deacon Freman invited Annie to come to his house for an Amway meeting. Annie knew that he was a widower and remembered when his wife died three years earlier. She said she would attend and when she arrived Deacon Freeman directed her to sit on the sofa by him. There were other people present as well. One, in particular, was a woman in a house dress with curlers in her hair. Annie assumed she was Deacon Freeman's girlfriend and so, was puzzled as to why he asked her, Annie, to sit beside him. She continued to be puzzled as to why, when at church, he would talk to her about Ander's clothing, he always said that he wanted to come to one of Ander's baseball games. Finally, one day, Annie told him when the next game was, and he came. During the game, he asked Annie to have dinner with him. They began dating pretty often and continued for about three months. Since Annie did not believe in sex outside marriage, when he asked her to marry him, she said, "Yes". Although Annie was not madly in love with Bill, as she called him, she thought he was a good man. She knew that he was twenty years older than she was, but she thought they could have a comfortable relationship. Bill had seven adult children. He arranged for them to meet Annie and Ander before the simple wedding which they had one Saturday afternoon at church.

Since Annie and Bill wanted to attend a seven-day church retreat that Annie had planned, they took Ander to Mt. Union to stay with his grandparents for two weeks. Ander was good friends with the kids living nearby. They, in turn, loved it when Ander came, because he always had the latest video games. Moses and Maggie's house was full of kids when Ander was in town. Maggie knew what foods he liked and was sure to cook them.

Ander was eleven years old at the time, and like other growing boys, he loved to eat. When Annie and Bill returned to take Ander back home, Annie saw he had gained weight. After coming home, Ander continued gaining weight. When Annie realized that he had gained thirty pounds over a six-week period, she took him to the pediatrician's office. The doctor said he was depressed and told Annie that he needed to be under the care of a psychiatrist. He gave her the name of one in the area.

Annie always kept in close contact with Ander's teachers. Ander was a sensitive impressionable kid. One night, after Annie put him to bed, he woke up crying. When Annie asked him why he was crying, he said the teacher had told him that she was going to kill him. Annie made one of her frequent trips to the school and let the teacher know how upset he was over her threat to "string him up". Unfortunately, the teacher said Ander had to learn the difference between literal and figurative speech. The more professional teachers had less trouble with Ander. Others were always on the telephone, complaining about his behavior. The year he was in sixth grade, he complained that the kids "picked" on him. Annie paid the teacher a visit. Some of the words he used in talking about the other kids led Annie to think that they were racially motivated. When she talked to the teacher, the teacher said that he was known, not as "the black kid", but as the "fat kid". Annie brought this to the attention of his psychiatrist. When she did, he made an attempt to refer them to a behaviorally motivated dietician.

One afternoon, about this time, Annie came home from work to find Ander lying on the floor in the dining room, hitting his head on the floor. Bill was nearby in the kitchen. He told Annie that Ander was upset about something. When Annie tried to talk to Ander, nothing he said made sense. Annie told Bill that they had better take him to the emergency room. On the way there, as Annie sat in the back seat with Ander, he began yelling, "Mom, Dad, get down. They are shooting at us". Annie tried to calm him down, to no avail. He was examined by the doctor. He gave him orange juice. The doctor asked Annie if he had taken any drugs. She said, "No". Ander seemed to settle down after drinking the juice. They soon left, stopping at a nearby restaurant to get cheese steaks.

Ander had a pretty uneventful night, but on awakening, he was quite irrational. Annie gave him orange juice. He calmed down. Annie decided that there was no way that she could go to work that day. She called and lied and said that she was sick. She decided to take Ander to the psychiatrist. As they were going there, Ander got more and more depressed. As they were walking to the office, Ander kept saying that he wanted to kill himself. When they saw the psychiatrist, Annie decided it was not a good fit and took Ander to a clinic connected to a hospital near where they lived. This physician thought Ander needed to be hospitalized. He was admitted to the Children's Heart Hospital. He was given medication and put on a low-calorie diet.

Ander was not happy there. Nevertheless, he did stay there for two weeks. His condition improved, so Annie re-enrolled him in school. He remained depressed, however. One day, when Annie was home, since her classes were over, the principal brought Ander home at the end of the school day. He had not realized that Annie was home. Ander had been sleeping all day in school. When his teacher took him to the principal's office, he let him sleep there. Ander continued to be very drowsy at home. Only later did Ander tell Annie that he had taken one of her pills, (Elavil). After that, she kept her medications under lock and key.

During the rest of sixth grade, Annie took Ander to the clinic. He had to miss half a day of school each week, but his health was important. As he prepared to go to seventh grade, where he would have to go from room to room for his classes, Annie tried to have him visit this psychiatrist in the evening. The doctor refused, however, and would only agree to seeing Ander during the day. Annie got the message. She had been through this all before when they had been referred only to black physicians in the city of Philadelphia.

Annie had worked with a particular psychiatrist one summer, when she was the nurse for a Head Start program. She was impressed with how he had treated mentally challenged families, by policing their diets. Annie knew that Ander's illness was biochemical in nature. Sure enough, Dr. Ellis took Ander off many foods, including cow's milk. When Annie took him to see this doctor as long as Ander stuck to his diet, his behavior improved. Annie talked to Ander about his diet and he learned what foods to avoid. With this knowledge and with medication, as Ander got into his teenage years, and with deciding to work after school, Ander was very happy throughout these years.

CHAPTER FORTY-THREE

Annie and Bill's marriage only lasted eighteen months: Bill thought he could use Annie as a punching bag. After two episodes of being beat, one time, where she had to leave the house overnight. Annie gave up. The last straw came when Annie had to be hospitalized for severe radiculopathy and worsening of her MS. Ander was at home with Bill. One night when Annie came back into her room from the waiting room, her roommate told her that her phone had been ringing. Annie called home. Bill told her that "Ander jumped out the window". He then told her that the police were there, and they were going to find him. For some reason, Ander had become frightened of Bill. Ander went upstairs, leaving Bill downstairs. He then made a rope out of his bedclothes and climbed out of the window. Annie decided, then and there, that it was time for Bill to go. It was one thing for her to be afraid of Bill but she could not let Ander be afraid of him. So, after contacting their pastor, she told Bill to leave. Annie planned to file for divorce. However, shortly after Bill left, she found out that he was ill and thought it would be cruel to file when he was sick. Three years later, he died, leaving Annie a widow.

CHAPTER FORTY-FOUR

The first three years of Annie's disability retirement was a harrowing period. She was hospitalized a total of thirteen times, mostly because of severe back pain. But as well, she had abdominal surgery for removal of her gallbladder and repair of a hiatal hernia. At one-point, Annie also developed bleeding ulcers. Moses and Maggie came to stay a couple of weeks with Ander. He was now sixteen years old. During some hospitalizations, he was at home during the day and at night stayed with trustworthy neighbors. Ander worked at Wendy's part-time, after school and on weekends.

Annie was dismayed to find out that Dorothy had told everyone that the Army physicians said her back pain was just in her head. That explained why no one in the family took Annie's illness very seriously, even when physicians later said it was the first manifestation of Multiple Sclerosis. Annie thought some of the lack of concern was because of the fact that, while Annie had been able to show her siblings how to deal with many things in their lives, she could not show them how to deal with a sick older sister. For example, John only visited Annie three times during the thirteen hospitalizations, even though he was nearby. Annie knew that John was also dealing with personal problems and so forgave him for back of attention.

It was during the first year of her disability that Annie began thinking of moving to Florida. She noticed that her condition improved during the spring and summer months. Also, once in April, 1978, when Annie and the rest of the family drove to South

Carolina for their grandparents' funerals, the back pain practically went away. Of course, Moses and Maggie were dead set against her moving to Florida. Annie put off moving, also, because Moses was not well.

Finally, after spending a month in the VA hospital and being in bed on morphine for all of the winter of 1989-1990, Annie knew she had to do something. The move to Florida seemed to be the answer, and she started making tentative plans. Ander was in his second year of college in Virgina, and he said he would never move to Florida. It stayed on Annie's mind, however, and she started researching the move.

During one of Annie's hospitalizations, she had a huge argument with Dr. Kenton, the neurologist who diagnosed her as having MS. When he wanted to admit Annie, he told her that he thought she had a herniated disc in her lower back. When the myelogram showed no disc, he became very angry and said that he still thought she had MS, but said that it was in remission, even though she had the same symptoms that she had when he first diagnosed that illness. During his outburst, he told Annie that he had filled out more forms for her than he had for any other patient. What he seemed to forget was that he had charged Annie twenty dollars for every form that he filled out even for the ones that he only had to duplicate. Apparently, Dr. Kenton was afraid he was going to have to justify Annie remaining on disability.

With all the disputes and possible mismanagement that Annie had to endure, it was not surprising that she became depressed and ended up under the care of a psychiatrist, although she had resisted seeing one. She told one of her doctors that it was because she did not know what to talk to him about. The doctor, in turn told her to talk about her pain. When Annie saw Dr. Williams, the psychiatrist, she found she had plenty to say to him. Also, he helped her deal with her pain by teaching her biofeedback and she was able to use it to diminish her pain. Annie was even able to reduce her blood pressure, using this technique.

CHAPTER FORTY-FIVE

About this time Annie met Neal Ford. He lived about seventy miles from her and didn't mind driving that distance to see her. Neal worked at a can manufacturing company factory and had a different day off, usually during the week. He knew that Annie was disabled and didn't seem to mind. At times, Annie would lie down on the back seat when they went out. He did not mind that. When they were at home, Annie, at times, would lay on the floor, as she had less pain lying on a hard surface. Neal took her to Atlantic city, at times, where they took advantage of lower mid-week prices at the hotel casinos, there. They would spend the day at the indoor pool and spa and then see a play and have dinner in the evening. Since Moses was sick, Neal even drove Annie to MT Union, where they spent the weekend with her parents. Jim and Shirley, his wife, spent that weekend in Mt. Union, as well. Neal stayed at their vacation home. Maggie had a rule that if you weren't married, your boyfriend or girlfriend could not stay in their house with you. She was so overwhelmed at Neal's thoughtfulness at bringing Annie to see her sick father, however, that she was going to break this rule for him. Fortunately, Jim and Shirley, knowing Mother's rule, invited Neal to spend the night at their house.

CHAPTER FORTY-SIX

For some time now, Annie had felt that the Lord was calling her to preach the gospel. She talked to Rev. Pollard, her pastor about it. He told her that if the Lord was calling her that she had better respond. Although Annie had two Master's degrees and one Doctoral degree, Rev. Pollard encouraged her to get a Master's in Religion or a Divinity degree. Annie revisited the suggestion and thought that since she had so much education, she could do self-study and not get any further degrees. Periodically, she discussed the situation with Rev. Pollard.

After Annie decided to put plans in motion to move to Florida, she talked to Rev. Pollard. She told him about her sick father and that she wanted to at least become licensed while her father was alive. Reluctantly Rev. Pollard consented to letting Annie preach her trial sermon, which was necessary for becoming licensed to preach the gospel. She was overjoyed that she could finally put the wheels in motion to do so. The trial sermon was scheduled for July 29, 1990. At first, Rev. Pollard wanted Annie to preach the morning sermon, however he found out it was Women's Day and another speaker had already been scheduled. That made it necessary to schedule Annie to preach at the afternoon service.

Moses was getting sicker. In May, Annie and Ander drove to Mt. Union to see him. He was in the hospital. Maggie was very concerned about him. His doctor told her in December that he had cancer. When everyone met on Christmas Day at Dorothy's house

LESSONS IN LOVING

in Baltimore, Maggie discussed the diagnosis with everyone then. This she did out of Moses' hearing as she did not want to let him know his diagnosis. Now that he was getting sicker, she did not know what to do. Being a nurse, Annie knew that she had to help her father face his oncoming death. She did this, not only during visits, but also through letters and phone calls.

All of Moses' and Maggie's kids made it a point to visit them more often as Moses got sicker. Maggie was relieved to find out from one of their sons that Moses had approached his doctor about his diagnosis, and the doctor told Moses he had cancer. Maggie was also worried about what she should do about the issue of resuscitation if Moses' heart should stop. After discussing it with her children, she made the decision not to resuscitate if and when Moses' heart stopped. Maggie was much relieved after making the decision.

During his last weeks in the hospital, at least one or two of Moses' children were with him at all times. Therefore, when he left this earth, there was a son, a daughter, a daughter-in-law, and Maggie present at his bedside. His remaining children, his brothers, and sisters visited the week before he died. His funeral was one of the largest in Mt. Union. People attended from all over the eastern seaboard and as far away as South Carolina, where he was born and raised. Moses died exactly three weeks and two days before Annie preached her trial sermon. The event was attended by Maggie and most of Annie's brothers and sisters, as well as a few aunts, uncles and cousins. Moses was missed by all attending, as commented on by Annie during her sermon.

CHAPTER FORTY-SEVEN

Annie completed steps of her upcoming move to Florida. Ander was at home for the summer. This summer, as with all summers, he worked full time, making enough money to buy clothing and to save for spending money for the school year, when he would not be working. Since he stayed off campus, Annie allowed him to take some of his furniture back with him. She had to arrange for a moving van to move the rest of her furniture to Florida. Annie made a trip there in April. She first decided to move to Port Charlotte, where a friend, whom she met through her civilian federal job, had moved a few years previously. But she stayed in Bradenton in April and liking it better, decided to move there. Bradenton was in the southwestern part of Florida, right on the Gulf of Mexico. There was an international airport between Bradenton and Sarasota. Being in the southern part of Florida, the year-round temperature was in the middle seventies, although it could be as high as 95*F in the summer and as cold as 60*F in January.

When Annie was first diagnosed as having MS in 1979, (although her neurologist thought her onset was in her early twenties when she was in the Army Nurse Corps), she researched her illness and found that swimming was thought to delay the progression of the disease. Thus, Annie then signed up for a series of swimming lessons at the local YMCA and learned to swim. She then had an inground pool installed in her back yard at her house in Delaware County. She tried to have it covered and heated so that she could swim year-round. However, county regulations did not allow for the type of cover she had. Nevertheless, she swam all summer in her pool and as much as she could in the winter in enclosed pools. The move to Florida would allow her to swim year-round. In Florida, Annie was able to find an apartment complex, where there was a community pool. She hoped to find a house with a pool as soon as possible.

Neal offered to drive Annie's car to Florida when he had consecutive days off. Annie was not strong enough to drive that far. She readily accepted Neal's offer and made arrangements to fly to Bradenton the first week in September 1990. She felt extremely bad to be moving so far away from her recently widowed mother, but had already discussed with Maggie the possibility of her coming to Florida to spend January and February rather than to be snowed in through the winter in MT Union. Maggie said she would think about it. So, it came about that three years after becoming disabled Annie was off to Florida to live permanently.

CHAPTER FORTY-EIGHT

Within two weeks of arriving in Bradenton, Annie's furniture arrived and she settled into her two-bedroom apartment. It was situated on a lake and the pool was about two blocks from Annie's apartment. She drove there daily. Annie contacted a realtor and began looking at houses. Not knowing whether or not she would end up in a wheelchair, she directed her attention toward houses that were assessible. She thought that she probably would have to have a house built and so at first looked at sample houses. One day, while scanning the newspaper, Annie came upon an ad for a wheelchair house. She immediately contacted her real estate agent, and they went to look at the house. Much to Annie's delight the house was exactly what she wanted. It had been built by a veteran who was paraplegic. It was ranch style and had low ramps leading to the front door and in the garage. There was an inground pool with three steps into the shallow end. The house had three bedrooms and two bathrooms, within Annie's price range. It was situated on a quiet street in a development, not too far from two shopping centers. Annie was glad that she did not have to wait to have a house built and signed the contract right away. Settlement was set for the end of January 1991.

Annie's real estate agent directed her to a Baptist church where Annie attended most every Sunday, and she knew several people there. She also found banks and grocery stores near her apartment.

The house was not far from her apartment complex, making it so that Annie did not have to get used to a whole new neighborhood.

CHAPTER FORTY-NINE

As promised, Neal drove Annie's car to Florida the first chance that he had four consecutive days off. While he was down there, they visited a home show. Neal pushed Annie in her wheelchair as the building in which it was held, was quite a large one. Neal also wanted to visit One Buc Place, the headquarters for the Tampa Bay Buccaneers (football). He didn't seem to mind pushing Annie, so they visited both places. He then flew back to Pennsylvania at the end of the weekend.

That year, Annie flew to Philadelphia for Thanksgiving, where Ander met her. They rented a car and drove to MT Union. Annie and her seven brothers and sisters and their families arranged to meet for Thanksgiving dinner in MT Union at Jim and Shirley's vacation home. They wanted to spend Thanksgiving together with their Mother, as this was the first Thanksgiving that their father was gone and they wanted to spend it together in his honor. Mamadou prepared a plate of food, putting it outside for Moses' spirit. This was an old Native American custom. Maggie said nothing, and it was evident by her silence that she didn't believe in the custom. Nevertheless, everybody had a good time and were happy to see each other in better circumstances than the last time they had been together in MT Union.

The day before Christmas, Dorothy and her husband Matt drove to MT Union to get Maggie. The next day they, along with Maggie and their two daughters, boarded the train to Orlando,

Florida. Ander, who was at home for semester break, drove with Annie to Orlando, where they met Dorothy and her family, and Maggie. They all spent several days sightseeing at Disney World and Epcot Center. Thereafter, Ander drove Annie and Maggie back to Bradenton. Maggie stayed with Annie for two months, avoiding spending the winter alone in MT Union.

Maggie enjoyed her two months in Florida. She got a chance to meet Annie's friends as well as to attend church with Annie. She also heard her speak at a couple of the churches. Maggie was relieved to see Annie's health improve, making it possible for her to do what she felt the Lord was calling her to do: preach the gospel! All too soon the two months were over. Annie arranged for her housekeeper to accompany her to Tampa where they put Maggie on the train to go back to Baltimore, where Dorothy and Matt met the train and drove her to MT Union. This was the longest time Maggie had ever been away from home. She planned to spent the next winter in Florida as well and did so for a total of four winters.

CHAPTER FIFTY

Annie continued adjusting to life in Florida. It was a blessing not to have to worry about driving in the ice and snow. She was able to find a lady to come three times a week, helping her with the housework, grocery shopping and driving. Annie hired her through a county organization, being paid one half of the first six weeks' pay, which they considered the length of time need to train her. Mary Lou, the lady's name, was a cheerful older woman, who had just buried her partner of eleven years. He had been her major source of income, and now with him gone, she had to find employment. She came to help Annie on Mondays, Wednesdays, and Fridays. Annie had required this type of help since 1978. Annie was just happy that she did not have to go into a nursing home.

Annie continued speaking at churches as her health permitted. At one church she attended, the lead pastor wanted her to conduct services at 8:30AM and 11AM. Annie did this for two Sundays but found that it was too much for her and she had to give up the position. Annie found that it was necessary to pace herself, as she was very easily fatigued.

Neal continued to visit Annie and spent part of his vacation in Florida. On one occasion, they had a big disagreement: Neal was pushing Annie in her wheelchair. At one point he let go of it as they were going downhill. Annie snapped at him, saying, "You have to learn how to push my wheelchair". Neal replied "No, I don't!" Annie got very angry and said very little for a whole day. Neal later apologized, and they made up, after he said he was wrong to let the wheelchair go. The whole situation stayed on Annie's mind, however.

Ander was still going to school in Virginia. He chose to live with his father, Thad, during the summer of 1991. He thought that he could find a job easier in Philadelphia than in Florida. He worked, delivering pizzas the first part of the summer and, later, got a job at the post office. He had one more year to go before he could graduate.

One day when Ander was in class at Virginia State, he was called out of class by a university official. A previous student, Darlene Bailey, was there with her four-month-old baby. She told Ander that he was her baby's father. Ander found it hard to believe, although he had dated Darlene briefly during the Fall semester. Since Ander was slow in accepting that he was the father of Ishear, the baby's name, Darlene, somehow, obtained Annie's address. She began writing her and sending pictures. She said she did not want money, but only wanted her son to know his people. Annie accepted the letters and studied the pictures. Iddy, as Darlene called him, looked surprisingly like Ander at that age. Annie discussed the situation with Ander. Gradually Ander accepted that Idi was his son and began seeing him. Annie did not meet Idi until he was four years old. He was a sweet little boy and the only grandchild that Annie had. As the years went by, Ander included Idi in family gathering, assuring that he did 'know his people'.

CHAPTER FIFTY-ONE

One afternoon Annie and Maggie were talking as they often did when she was visiting Annie. Maggie told Annie how she had remained a virgin while Moses was "courting" her. She said she knew that Moses visited other women to get the sex that she was not giving him. Annie became upset, saying, "I don't want to hear anything like that about my father!" Maggie got up and went to her room. When she came out later that day, she was subdued and wearing both her and Moses' wedding rings. Annie now wished that she had been able to talk to Maggie about her father and other women.

Annie took a nap that afternoon also. When she awakened, she couldn't move. She often had these spells, where she would be awake, but unable to move a single muscle. She had talked to her mother about these occurrences. She had never read about anything like them. Maggie told Annie that, "The witches are riding you." After lying in bed for a few minutes, she would become fully awake and able to move. It was a horrible feeling to lie there, half awake, and unable to move. It was almost like she was paralyzed. That afternoon was the last time she ever experienced that feeling again. Somehow it seemed to Annie that she had the occurrences more when she was around her mother. Try as she might, she could not figure it out. It remained a mystery.

CHAPTER FIFTY-TWO

Ander began to have more problems at college. One day he called Annie to tell her that he had found out that a boy who had been a good friend of his since nursey school, had killed himself. Ander was very upset and called Annie several times that day. Annie told him to be sure to eat because she knew he was likely to forget to eat and would become more stressed out. She called the parents of the friend, Sammie and found out that the funeral had been the day before.

The next day Ander was still upset. Coming out of class, he saw his car being towed away. He ran to get a knife out of his car and cut the towing ropes and the school officials had him Baker Acted and notified Annie. She got in touch with the hospital, giving them the insurance information and checking on his condition. Annie knew she needed to go there and made arrangements to do just that. By the time she got there, 2 days later, Ander had been discharged from the hospital, but was still shakened.

That year was rough on Ander. Although Annie stayed at the college for two weeks and talked to the school psychologist on several occasions, he was still arrested for the incident concerning the tow truck. Annie bailed him out and he continued with his classes. However, later, there was an incident where Ander wrestled a paper out of the hand of a clerk. Finally, the school lawyer said that if Ander was going to continue there, he had to be under the care of a psychiatrist, attend Narcotic Anonymous meetings and attend

Batters Anonymous meetings. Annie agreed to provide him with these requirements. Ander went to summer school that summer. He planned to finish his requirements for his degree by December 1992. He visited Annie on the break between Spring semester and summer school. Annie was ready to contact a psychiatrist to treat Ander, when one day in the summer, she got a call from the school lawyer. She said Ander had taken food from the cafeteria without paying for it. The lawyer said they were suspending him for a year and Ander had to leave the school property immediately. Ander and Annie were in close contact as he handed in his last paper for his summer school classes and left the school.

CHAPTER FIFTY-THREE

Annie had been spending her summers in MT Union ever since she moved to Florida, thus avoiding the intensively hot weather. In the summer of 1992, she flew to Baltimore and met Ander there. He had left Virginia State University and had spent a few days with his Aunt Dorothy and her family. When Annie arrived in Baltimore, she and Ander joined his Uncle Ben, who took them to MT Union. They spent two enjoyable months there with Maggie, at the end of which they joined Maggie and another of Annie's sisters, Helaine and Melanie, her daughter on a trip to New York City. Annie wanted to see a play on Broadway, plus she and Ander planned to start a business in Florida, and they needed to buy supplies.

Annie thought it was better that Ander not be under the pressure of working under someone else, as his condition was not stable at the time. While in New York, Annie's brother, Mamadou, took them to wholesale shops where they bought fabric, books, jewelry, and other items which they could sell at flea markets and festivals in Florida. Mamadou had a similar business in NYC and knew of many suitable outlets.

After spending a few days with Helaine and her family, Annie and Ander visited Jim and his family in a Washington, DC suburb for a week. Since Annie lived so far from them, the rest of her brothers and sisters wanted her to spend as much time as possible with them, while she was up North for the summer. Annie agreed to spend time with them on the condition that they visit her in Florida. They were a very close family.

CHAPTER FIFTY-FOUR

Annie and Ander returned to Florida and went about the task of organizing and building a business. First, they decided on a name for their business. Ander suggested 'So Unique' but upon researching names on the internet found that name to be in use. Ander suggested adding another "o" to So, but Annie said people would pronounce that as "sue", which she didn't like. She suggested adding two "o's"; so, the business was called Sooo Unique so it would be pronounced with an elongated "o".

They next set up a mailbox at a UPS store. While there, they had business cards made, including all the pertinent information about the business, such as the name, address, email address, and their phone numbers. They also filed the necessary paper work for a fictitious name along with filling out the forms necessary for collecting state sales tax.

Both Annie and Ander were excited about the business and had fun selling. In 1992 all things African were popular. While they were in New York City, Annie and Ander bought yards upon yards of African Kente cloth. They sold the actual fabric, but also learned to sew African clothing, including dashiki's, kufi's, and pants. They also bought dolls and made African clothing for them. They ordered catalogs for prints and photographs. They also made jewelry. They went to thrift shops and found items there that they knew would sell.

Next on their agenda was finding places to sell their merchandise. This they did by reading newspapers daily and keeping up with different festivals in their area. They also sold at flea markets nearby. One weekend, they even traveled to North Carolina to attend a three-day festival. Items they sold were popular; they had no problem selling them. A Nigerian friend of Annie's made a trip to visit his mother in Nigeria. Annie gave him money to buy carvings of wooden masks. Business was booming, and Annie was pleased that Ander had a knack for selling. Many nights, after she had gone to bed, Ander stayed up sewing or making jewelry.

CHAPTER FIFTY-FIVE

Toward the end of December, Ander got the idea of contacting his school in Virginia to see if he could take his remaining four courses in Florida. They gave him verbal permission. He enrolled at the University of South Florida in Tampa, which was fifty miles from Bradenton. He started school there and did the business on weekends.

Since Ander had been in Florida, he suffered one big problem. He was always being stopped by the police while driving. He learned several different routes home, trying to avoid them. They never arrested him but continued stopping him. He would show them his driver's license and they would let him go. One day, Annie sent Ander to the store. When it was about time for him to come home, Annie heard sirens. Immediately Annie guessed correctly that it was the police following Ander. Sure enough, when she looked out the window, she saw Ander pulling into the driveway. A police car was pulling in behind him. Annie went outside. Ander started to get out of the car. The police woman told him to stay in the car. This he did. The police woman got out of her car. Annie said to her, "Why are you all always stopping him?" She said, "He was going a little fast. Maybe there is something wrong with the speedometer." After she looked at his license, she got back in her car, not giving Ander a ticket. Annie was infuriated. She decided to call police headquarters to complain about the problem. She talked to a Major there and shared her concerns with him. He said he would "talk to his officers."

CHAPTER FIFTY-SIX

One quiet Sunday in April 1993, Ander worked on a paper due the next day for one of the courses he was taking at USF. Annie spent the day reading in her room. Around 6PM, Ander told her that he was going to the library to type the paper. Shortly after 8PM, Ander called Annie to tell her that he had had an automobile accident and that he had been arrested. Apparently, he had stopped at friends' house and when told they were fishing, He went to find them. He saw them fishing in a small stream in West Bradenton. A policeman approached them and began asking to see ID's. Ander decided that, rather than show the cop his ID, he would just leave and got in his car. He turned his head to back up. When he turned back forward he saw the cop hanging on to the side mirror of the car. Ander panicked and kept going backward. Somehow, the car turned over on its side, causing the cop scratches and bruises. Other police were called and Ander was arrested.

Annie called a friend, Ed, to go with her to bail Ander out. They went downtown to a bail bonds man's office. He checked with the jail. No bond had been set. Annie and Ed returned to Annie's home. Ed decided to spend the night, and they would go back there the next day. Thus, Annie was not alone when Ander called her again round 12 midnight to tell her that there was no bail and that he was charged with attempted murder. Annie started to cry. Ed comforted her as much as possible. Somehow, Annie got through the night and was able to sleep for a few hours.

The following day, Annie called an attorney and went downtown to the court house. Ander's bail had been set at $5,000, and she paid 10% of that, bailing Ander out. Later that day they went to the attorney's office. He said he would represent Ander for $15,000 and required a retainer of $5,000 right away. Annie was successful in borrowing some of the $5,000 from her sisters and brothers.

Later during the following week, Jim and Shirley, and her brothers visited Annie and Ander. Jim, an attorney, said that he didn't understand the charges as there was no "intent". Annie was just glad that they were there, lending emotional support. Her family always rallied around when there was trouble. They were a God send.

Ander's charges dragged on until the following spring. Ander was under the care of a psychologist, recommended by his attorney. Annie was hospitalized for five days at the Veteran Administration Hospital for depression. At one-point Ander was Baker Acted and spent three days in a psychiatric hospital. In the end, the charges were changed to a much lesser offence, and Ander was sentenced to eighteen months of probation. His attorney recommended that he not spend his probation in Bradenton. Ander arranged to stay with his Uncle Jim and his family in Maryland and his probation was transferred there.

CHAPTER FIFTY-SEVEN

Annie and Neal gradually drifted apart. They, at first, kept in touch by phone. However, the time between phone calls got longer and longer, until they finally ceased altogether. In 1992, Annie met Ed, a Nigerian man, through mutual friends. One evening, she was part of a group who went to ST Petersburg to see a play. Ed was the only male member of the group and he and Annie became romantically involved right away. Ed was the third Nigerian boyfriend that Annie had had. Lawrence, whom Annie met while she was attending Penn, was the first. Steve, an auditor for a major shoe manufacturing company, was the second. Although Ed was twenty-four years younger than Annie he possessed a certain cosmopolitan air that Annie found interesting. He liked to do some of the same things that she did and they hit it off right away. Because of the age difference, Annie never thought of Ed as a suitable marriage partner. He was a nice boyfriend, however. Another reason why marriage was out of the question was that Ed wanted children and Annie was unable to have any. Nevertheless, they enjoyed spending time with each other.

Ander had had no trouble finding a job in Maryland and when he visited Annie, he liked Ed right away. Perhaps because they were so close in age.

Annie continued speaking at different churches. She presently attended "The Tabernacle of Prayer and Deliverance" and the pastor there, Rose Morton, licensed her to preach in Florida. On the property where the church was located there was a small house where Pastor Morton's daughter had a hair salon. One day, on leaving the salon, Annie fell down the flight of five steps. Initially she experienced no pain. However, a month later, she became unable to put any weight on her left leg, the side on which she fell. Upon visiting an orthopedic surgeon and being X-rayed, the finding was a left hip fracture. The orthopedic surgeon initially planned to do a hip pinning but had to remove the entire hip, replacing it, when the pinning screws would not hold. Annie's hope for a quick recovery was filled with one complication after another, including an infection and repeated loosening of the prosthesis, resulting in five years of repeated surgeries. She even went to Philadelphia to have one surgery. Finally, an orthopedic surgeon at Blake Hospital in Bradenton did a relatively new surgery, where he did both a hip replacement and a knee replacement, thus anchoring the hip.

CHAPTER FIFTY-EIGHT

When Annie's health permitted it, she enjoyed cruising. The first cruise that Annie took was in 1995, when her close friend and cousin Anna Jane (nicknamed Betty Mae) asked her to accompany her on a cruise, where they would fly to Puerto Rico and then cruise all the way down the Caribbean Sea to Caracas Venezuela and back. They were part of a group from Trenton, New Jersey, where Betty Mae lived, which included two more cousins, Phyllis and Monica, and their beloved Uncle Frank, the last remaining of Moses' brothers. Six months later Annie and Helaine cruised down the Northern Carribean stopping at different islands than before. Several years later, Annie cruised alone down the Atlantic Ocean to Costa Rica. Then, when Ander moved back to Florida, he and Annie cruised again in the Carribean for 12 days. By using an electric scooter, Annie was able to manipulate the long corridors and many elevators on the ship.

Next, Annie plans to travel to Los Angeles, California and then later, perhaps, a cruise to Alaska. It would be nice to find someone to accompany her on these trips. Although, she made friends easily when traveling, it was always more fun to travel with someone.

CHAPTER FIFTY-NINE

One day in the summer of 1996 while Annie and Maggie were talking Maggie said, "I think I will write Neal a letter thanking him for all the cards he has been sending me over the years at Mother's Day and all. I am going to write him a letter, trying not to mention you." Because of this, Annie thought, "If you are going to write a letter without mentioning me, I'll write my own letter."

It happened that as Annie and Maggie were again talking one evening, the phone rang. Maggie picked up the phone and after saying, "Hello," got a puzzled expression on her face. When Annie asked her what was the matter, she said. "It was someone saying something about dinner." Annie right away knew who it was and when the phone rang a few minutes later, she answered it. Just as she thought, it was Neal. She had written him, telling him that she would be staying in MT Union for the summer and that he was welcome to visit. That call was the beginning of the renewal of Annie's and Neal's relationship. Neal was now retired and working at Walmart part-time. He started driving to MT Union every few weeks on his days off. They dated all summer and by August had decided to get married the following year. During the summer they went for long drives in the country enjoying the beautiful Appalachian Mountain ranges and valleys. They had plenty of time to talk. Neal told Annie that he had considered moving to Florida when she moved, but the closest factory that his company had, was in Jacksonville and that was twelve hours from Bradenton. Because of that he had not requested a transfer.

That Christmas, Neal spent ten days visiting Annie in Bradenton. They had been intimate during their prior relationship, but Annie told Neal that she wanted to wait until they were married to become intimate again. Reluctantly Neal agreed. During his visit, Annie experienced a lot of back pain. They spent most of the visit at home, going out to dinner only one time.

CHAPTER SIXTY

Annie spent most of the summer of 1997 planning her upcoming wedding. They planned to have an African wedding. Only family members are invited to this type of wedding. Annie and Neal planned to invite a few very close friends, however. Jim and Shirley consented to having the affair at their large Washington, DC suburban home. For the most part Annie's health remained good for most of the summer. However, she was hospitalized overnight for chest pain the day after accepting RSVP's all day.

Mamadou, Annie youngest brother, took Annie and Maggie to New York City to stay with him for a week, giving Annie a chance to shop for a suitable white dress for her African wedding. Maggie made a head dress for Annie to wear during the ceremony. Phillis, Annie's cousin from MT Union, took Annie to Altoona to shop, giving her a chance to buy white shoes.

Neal, Annie, and Maggie travelled together to Maryland two days prior to the wedding day. This gave Annie and Neal a chance to complete their pre-marital counseling, begun with the officiating minister. Mamadou, who was going to preside over the African part of the wedding, arrived a day early to rehearse. There was a huge discussion among all present at the house as to whether or not Mamadou should invite the spirits of dead relatives to be present, as Mamadou said was the custom in African weddings. The ending consensus was that he should not issue such an invitation.

The wedding day arrived! Annie got dressed at Jim and Shirley's home. The room was filled with her sisters, some sisters-in-law and Maggie. Annie could look out the window and see guests arriving and was not surprised to see approximately eighty people in Jim and Shirley's family room when Ander escorted her downstairs. Pastor Bennie completed his part of the ceremony, then it time for Mamadou's part. He started by having guests voluntarily announcing names of deceased relatives. Annie, knowing her brother well, thought that Mamadou probably summoned the deceased relatives' sprits after their names were announced. This he did not verbalize.

After Mamadou finished, Annie and Neal, then formed a receiving line, and greeted each guest. They were all relatives of either Annie's or Neal's except there was one of Neal's close friends from New Jersey and three of Annie's close friends from Pennsylvania. After the ceremony was over, Shirley invited the guests to utilize any and all parts of the downstairs and basement, including the living room, family room, library, patio, and terrace. They enjoyed themselves for the next six hours. A three-piece band supplied live entertainment. The guests were treated to a full course buffet meal catered by associates of Jim and Shirley.

All in all, it was a very nice day. At the end of the evening, Annie felt pleasantly tired but felt in no distress. Soon after the last guest left, she and Neal went back to the hotel. Annie was surprised when Neal made no attempt at intimacy that night. He only awakened her at 3AM to tell her that Princess Diana had died.

Helaine had invited all the wedding quests to a brunch the next day starting at 10AM, since many of the guests were from out of town and were planning to stay overnight. Neal and Annie planned to attend, but took their time getting dressed and driving to Helaine's house in a different Maryland suburb. They got there about 11:30AM and socialized with Annie's immediate family for the rest of the day. Annie's brothers and sisters always enjoyed being together, and since the next day was Labor Day, they spent it together as well. In the evening, Annie and Neal drove Maggie back to MT Union. The next day they set out for Neal's house in Allentown, Pennsylvania.

Neal's house consisted of two bedrooms, a living room, kitchen and bath. Annie was surprised when Neal directed her to one of the bedrooms and then said he was going to sleep downstairs on the sofa. They planned to spend two weeks in Allentown and then drive to Florida. They spent the rest of the week shopping. On Saturday, Neal suggested a drive-in movie. At the movie, Neal was distant, he had been so all week. While dating Annie that summer and last summer, he had been very affectionate, kissing and hugging Annie frequently. Since they had been married, this affection was non-existing. When they got home from the drive-in, Annie attempted to hug Neal. He pushed her away so hard that Annie felt pain in her back. Annie was deeply hurt and started to cry, retreating to her room upstairs. Later that night, Neal came upstairs, saying he wanted to talk to Annie. He told Annie that he suffered from "premature ejaculation", and that he could not maintain an erection. Annie was very upset and started to cry again. She said he should have told her sooner. She remembered that when they had first gotten back together, Neal had wanted to be intimate but had reluctantly agreed to wait. When and with whom he found out that he could no longer perform, were the first questions that entered Annie's mind. She told Neal that it was a big disappointment and that she had been looking forward to having sex with him after marriage. She was hurt that Neal had not told her the truth and also because he had been so distant since they had been married. The kissing and hugging that existed when they were engaged was now totally missing. This state of affairs continued. Neal treated Annie as a platonic friend, not as a wife whom he loved and even wanted to touch. It was not only a sexless marriage. It was also a loveless marriage.

The pain that Annie experienced when Neal pushed her away when they got home from the movies got worse. When they got back to Florida, she was hospitalized for two weeks and treated with potent pain medication (Demerol). When the neurologist discharged Annie, he neglected to prescribe any medication. When Annie was still up North, one of the anesthesiologists at the VA Hospital treated Annie's back pain by injecting steroids into her spinal canal. She could find no doctor to treat her this way in Florida. Annie began an unending quest for a physician who would prescribe the type of pain treatment she needed. One neurologist told Annie that she needed a morphine pump and gave her a list of physicians to contact. Annie contacted them all with no success. Neal would take her to a doctor's office and while the doctor examined and questioned Annie, Neal sat in the room with Annie, acting unconcerned, many times with his eyes closed. The doctors were naturally puzzled by his behavior and so did not take Annie seriously when she tried to explain the severity of her back pain. Needless to say, no physician agreed to implant a morphine pump.

CHAPTER SIXTY-ONE

Annie and Neal continued in their affectionless marriage. At this point, Annie was practically bedridden because of her pain. Neal usually spent every day out. He got up early each day and left. Sometimes, Annie would not even know when he left, as they slept in separate rooms. He usually came back around 6PM, spoke to Annie then retired to another room to watch television, leaving Annie alone in her room. One day, Neal told Annie that he had had a biopsy of his prostate gland and that he was due to get the results the next week. Annie forced herself out of bed, dressed and went with Neal to the doctor's office. The doctor told them that it was cancer and said that Neal needed surgery. Neal decided to delay the surgery until the summer when they went North. They decided to spend the summer in Allentown.

In the meantime, Annie continued visiting doctors, trying to obtain needed pain management. Once, she had to be Baker Acted, after she went to her next-door neighbor's house, saying her husband was trying kill her. Annie's mind was so wracked with pain she did not realize that she was nude. The stress from the unhappy marriage also was likely a contributing factor. Annie wanted to wait until she got the morphine pump and until Neal had his surgery before making any decision about their marriage. That way she felt that she would have given the marriage a fair chance.

CHAPTER SIXTY-TWO

In order to avoid the oppressive heat that characterized summers in Florida, Neal decided to drive to Pennsylvania in May 1998. Annie flew to Maryland two weeks later. Neal met her at the airport. They then drove to MT Union to spend Memorial Day weekend. Several of Annie's brothers and sisters and their families were scheduled to visit as well. Annie earlier proposed an idea to them about forming a non-profit family organization to help other families not as fortunate as theirs. On Saturday, all except one sister and one brother arrived. Unfortunately, there was a big argument between Annie and two of her sisters over sleeping arrangements at Maggie's house, thus erasing any chance of a family meeting. By Sunday evening everyone had gone home.

Next Annie and Neal traveled to Allentown. There, Neal slept downstairs on the sofa. Annie slept upstairs and after falling in the bathroom, injuring her hip, she left and checked into a motel. Neal visited her in the evenings watching television there. Soon, it was time for Neal's surgery. He had scheduled it at John Hopkins Hospital in Baltimore. He and Annie checked into a hotel there a few days before the surgery. There Annie went with Neal to visit the surgeon, when he told Neal what to expect pre- and postoperatively. He gave Neal written instructions as to how to resume sexual relations with his wife. They were both alert and attentive.

The surgical day soon arrived. Annie and Neal went by the hotel van to the hospital. That way, Annie would not have to drive back to the hotel alone. Annie stayed at the hospital all day. She was lying down in one of the postoperative waiting room when the surgeon came to tell her that the surgery had been successful and that Neal would soon be taken to his room. Annie was in severe pain; nevertheless, she went to Neal's room to wait. Shortly thereafter he returned. Neal was awake, but groggy and only half able to talk to Annie and his brother, Skip, who arrived shortly after he returned. After making sure Neal was comfortable, Annie accepted Skip's offer to take her back to the hotel.

Neal was discharged from the hospital at the end of the week. Since he was not allowed to drive for two weeks, he and Annie remained at the hotel. Twice during that week, Neal accompanied Annie to the emergency room, once at John Hopkins and once at ST Mary's Hospital; both times for pain out of control. Annie was admitted to ST Agnes Hospital toward the end of the two-week period. Since Annie became irrational, she was Baker Acted and admitted to a psychiatric hospital in the adjoining county. Annie remained there for a week, the end of which she was discharged, after proving that she was well enough to be treated as an outpatient. Neal came back from Allentown, where he had gone to check on the mail that weekend. Dorothy and her family, Helaine, and Jim and Shirley visited Annie in the psychiatric hospital while Neal was gone. They helped Annie celebrate her birthday with a cake that Sunday. Jim was present with Neal at the hearing when Annie proved her suitability for discharge.

The day after Annie was discharged from the hospital, Neal decided to return to Allentown. Annie did not accompany him. She wanted to stay in Baltimore for further treatment at the Veteran's Administrative Outpatient Clinic nearby. The day after Neal left, Ander arrived to stay with Annie. He was out of work and living with his girlfriend, Sharon, in Prince George, Maryland, having recently lost his job at Sprint Telephone Company. He was very depressed. Ander was also worried about Annie. Sharon arrived with him, but left after she and Annie argued. Annie did not like Sharon, as she had had Ander arrested for domestic abuse twice. Annie thought Sharon was lazy and that she did not like to work. Sharon had a five-year-old son, who was presently staying with her parents in New York City.

LESSONS IN LOVING

Annie and Ander moved to the Marriott Hotel. They stayed there a total of six weeks while Annie was undergoing treatment at the VA. Neal came back and stayed a few days. Finally, a doctor at the VA prescribed morphine for Annie and gave her a month's supply. Since she was finally getting treatment for her pain and since it was now September, Annie decided to return to Florida. Neal chose to stay in Allentown until November, however.

CHAPTER SIXTY-THREE

Since Annie's records had been returned to the VA in ST Petersburg from Balitmore, showing that her back pain was severe and required morphine to treat it. Annie expected VA doctors in ST Petersburg to continue ordering it for her. She was now classified as one hundred percent disabled and, along with Multiple Sclerosis, she also had a diagnosis of lumbar radiculopathy, a condition involving the spinal nerves in her low back.

On visiting the VA in October, Annie had no problem obtaining the morphine necessary to treat her pain. Ander was visiting her, and he not only drove her to ST Petersburg, but also remained at her bedside and told the doctors that she was bedridden due to pain. However, upon visiting the VA in November, when Neal took Annie, she was not so lucky. Neal did not remain with Annie, but stayed in the waiting room the entire five hours, while one doctor after another examined Annie, and at the end of that time, sent her home without any treatment. Annie even told them that she felt like going home and killing herself. They only became alarmed when she added that "First, I am going to come back here and take a few people with me."

Annie went home and got in bed. Her pain was now excruciating. It left like the nerves in her back were being burned with electric wires. She placed a bottle of sleeping pills on her bedside table. She considered taking all of them. She wondered if she would still have pain after she was dead. Annie decided to take one more action to try to receive some relief. She would ask Neal to take her to the local hospital emergency room. If he refused, she would take the pills. Neal consented to taking her to the emergency room. There she was given an injection of Demerol and a written prescription for Demerol tablets and told to see a private physician later. Annie went home, after Neal took her to an all-night pharmacy to have the prescription filled. Annie stretched the pills out over a long period so she could find a doctor to treat her. She was hurt that the physicians at the VA refused to give her any medicine. She injured her back way back in the early sixties, when she was an Army nurse, lifting children of Army personnel in and out of cribs which had sides that stuck when one tried to raise them. Now, as a veteran and suffering, she was denied treatment.

Annie had previously found one physician in Sarasota, who agreed to try a morphine pump on a temporary basis. It was routine to first insert a temporary pump to see if it helped and, second, to be sure that the patient was not allergic to it or the medication. This doctor did the minor surgery while Annie was an outpatient. He then sent her home. The dressings, which were holding the tube in her spinal column, came loose and pulled the tube out after it had been in for only ten hours. Annie felt much pain relief while the catheter was in place. When Annie returned to the doctor's office the next day, he became angry saying Annie had pulled the tube out on purpose and declined to treat her any further. Annie asked him to write a prescription for thirty days of morphine until she could make arrangements to see another doctor. He wrote the prescription.

Annie had also been treated by a doctor in Tampa, first as an outpatient with oral morphine, and then later with hospitalization for eight days where he installed a temporary morphine pump, promising her that he would implant a permanent pump after observing if the temporary one helped her. After fiddling with the pump for eight days and observing that it decreased Annie's pain, this doctor decided that he would not install a permanent pump unless Annie agreed to seeing another round of doctors, even though she had seen many consultants on a daily basis while in the hospital. Annie knew that this physician was simply stalling and so did not continue seeing him.

CHAPTER SIXTY-FOUR

Neal was Catholic and usually attended Mass every Friday. Annie went with him occasionally. Sometimes he would get up on Sunday morning and when Annie saw him getting dressed and ascertained that he was going to a Protestant church, she would go with him if she could. She knew that, most likely, during his travels and talking to people (as he always did), someone would invite him to attend their church. She thought that most likely it was a woman. When they returned to Florida, after their marriage, Neal had stopped wearing his wedding ring, stating that he was allergic to metal.

One evening when she was in her room watching television, with Neal being in a different room, Annie felt so lonely. Lately Neal had been talking about going North. The way he said it led Annie to know that he wanted to return there alone. Their marriage left a lot to be desired: Annie was spending more and more time alone. This night it came to her that it didn't make sense to be married and still be lonesome. She told Neal her feelings. He said he understood what she meant. Annie then told him that she wanted to end the marriage and by which date she wanted him to be gone. Neal agreed and began preparing to leave. They talked very little as the days went on. However, one-day Neal did ask Annie a question? He wanted to know if she was going to file for divorce or an annulment. Either would have been fitting since the marriage had not been consummated due to Neal's inability to perform. In Annie's mind, it was both his inability and/or his lack of desire. She had at one point mentioned Viagra to Neal. He said, "No, there is too much chance of having a heart attack." Annie told Neal she had not decided whether to file for a divorce or an annulment.

When Annie told her mother that she and Neal were separating, Maggie was not surprised. She said "Neal told me a year ago that he was tired, and that anyone can get tired." She said he told her a lot of other "stuff" that she wouldn't even repeat. This all made Annie know that she had come to the right decision. She only wished that Neal had told her that he was tired: He could have been resting for a whole year already.

All things considered, Annie and Neal had a pretty decent parting. As he stood in the doorway of Annie's room, talking, Annie said, "I think it's best to end this way." Neal replied, "I agree. You don't hear me saying anything, do you?" He then said "Goodbye," and got in his car and began the trip North, calling Annie a week later to inquire about items which Annie had left at his home in Allentown as to whether or not to send them. That was the last that Annie heard from Neal. Shortly thereafter she located an attorney and filed for divorce.

CHAPTER SIXTY-FIVE

Annie continued her search for a physician who would implant a permanent morphine pump. She was still bedridden with pain. Being desperate, Annie started visiting physicians whom she had already seen. One, who had declined to help her a year earlier, on the second visit (he didn't remember seeing her before) referred her to DR Steven Chun. DR Chun was the head of the pain program at Doctor's Hospital in Sarasota. After treating Annie with oral morphine for a month, DR Chun, deciding that Annie was someone who would benefit from a pump, hospitalized her and implanted a temporary pump. Annie did well with the temporary pump and without much fanfare, DR Chun implanted a permanent pump. He was a godsend. Annie was now able to be out of bed and was able to get on with her life.

For the last three years Annie had been unable to do any preaching. Now, since her pain was well managed, she began looking for a church where she could again preach the Word. While she was looking, Annie decided to take a trip North. It had been over a year since she had visited her mother. She also wanted to check on Ander. He was now living in Philadelphia. Although Thad, Ander's father, lived in Philadelphia, Ander preferred living on his own. He tried living with his father and his father's girlfriend; it had not worked, and he now lived in a one-bedroom apartment in North Philadelphia. Annie wanted him to travel to MT Union with her when she went to see her mother. Ander said he would go, but at the last minute decided not to.

During Annie's visit with Maggie she, upon attending church with her mother, asked her mother's pastor if she could preach that Sunday. The pastor said, "Yes," and Annie gave such a stirring message, that afterwards, everyone attending, gave her a hug or shook her hand, saying how well she did. It was good to go back 'home' and to be so well received. Maggie, of course, was overjoyed.

Upon going back to Philadelphia, prior to returning to Florida, Annie spent time with Ander. Something was up with him and on questioning him, she learned that he had started using crack cocaine. She was not surprised. She knew that forty percent of people, who are diagnosed as being bipolar, go on to use drugs. Annie tried to get Ander to go get help or to return to Florida with her. He refused to do either and Annie returned to Florida being very worried about him.

CHAPTER SIXTY-SIX

Annie had not been home long before Ander called her to tell her that he had been arrested. This began a period of one arrest after another, mostly for petty offenses. After spending time in jail, Ander would enter drug treatment programs, be clean for a while and then start the cycle all over again. It was a hard time for him.

One-day Ander called Annie to tell her that he had been arrested for conspiracy to sell drugs. He had been standing on the street late at night, when he was approached by two white males. Ander said they walked with him a short distance and then stopped. A black male, who was sitting in his car, got out and came to the three of them. He sold thirty dollars' worth of crack cocaine to the two white males. They gave Ander one of the bags of crack cocaine. The two white males turned out to be undercover policemen. They said Ander was working with the drug dealer. Ander said he was not and did not even know the man. Nevertheless, he was arrested. The lawyer that Annie retained for Ander took the case to trial. Ander was found guilty and sentenced to three and one-half years in prison and one year of probation. He served his time at a prison in upstate New York. Annie flew to New Jersey and visited Ander two different years, while he was there. Iddy, Ander's son, and his mother, Darlene Bailey, accompanied Annie. Collie, Darlene's adopted son, also went with them. They stayed at a hotel for two nights and visited Ander two days. He was in good spirits.

Ander spent most of his time in prison studying in a correspondence course. He also filed two lawsuits against the state of New York, one for forcing him to wear shoes that were three sizes too small, for a period of a week. The other lawsuit was against employees at the prison who had mistreated Ander while he was there. He was successful in both cases, receiving two thousand dollars for the first case and ninety-two thousand dollars for the second case. After he got out of prison and transferred his probation to Florida to be his mother's caretaker, he used some of the money to buy a house. He used his time in prison wisely.

Ander had first been exposed to Islam when he went away to college in 1988. While he was in prison he explored the religion more fully and while there became a practicing Muslim. When he moved to Bradenton he discovered that there was no mosque in Bradenton. Since Muslim men are required to pray five times a day, preferably at a mosque, Ander, with the help of three other Muslim men founded a mosque in Bradenton in 2013. He kept this mosque open and led meetings there for three years until he got sick again in 2016. His sickness was initiated by the death of his wife of two years, Margo Strachan. Ander remarried six months later to a woman whom he only knew for two days. This most likely was the reason the marriage only lasted one month. This, in turn, led to Ander falling off the wagon and again start using crack cocaine. When the police stopped Ander in his car, they found cocaine and arrested him. He was eventually sentenced to prison for sixteen months. He was very disappointed in himself. Annie was sorry that Ander's life was again disrupted by his illness and drug use. He was very depressed and had to be Baker Acted at one point. She tried her best to support him. He called her daily from the jail. She always made sure that he had money with which to buy items from the commissary. Ander was successful in finding a Muslim psychiatrist. Annie also paid for a private attorney for Ander and kept in close touch with him. Together, they faced the situation head on and it was not as bad as it could have been.

While Ander was in jail, Annie received a late-night call from Shameika Bailey, Iddy's sister, who told her that Iddy had been killed in a shoot-out with three armed men when they attempted to rob him. When Annie notified Ander the next day he, like Annie, was heartbroken. Since it would have required an exorbitant amount of money for Ander to travel to Iddy's funeral in New Jersey, both he and Annie were forced to do their grieving in Florida. They loved Iddy and found it hard to believe that he had been taken from them so soon. Ander had last seen Iddy in 2014. Annie had last seen him in 2011. They would miss him. He was only twenty-six years old. His girlfriend Janya, who shared his apartment, was present and was also killed. She was 5 months pregnant with Iddy's son.

CHAPTER SIXTY-SEVEN

Before Iddy was killed there had been a number of deaths in the Moses McCall family. Moses, the patriarch, succumbed to a long illness in 1990 at the age 81. When he was 47 years old he had spent one and a half years in a sanitorium for tuberculosis and silicosis brought on by his job of making bricks from silica sand. During his time at the sanitorium, Moses had two major surgeries where parts of both lungs were removed. Moses' brother, Ben, had died as a result of these two diseases. Knowing this to be a possible outcome of the diseases, Moses promised the Lord that if he would permit Moses to return home to his wife and kids that he would stop drinking. Having made this promise, when he did return to MT Union Moses did visit the "club" on a few occasions. However, it was not the same. He decided that that life was no longer one that he wanted to participate in. Therefore, Moses started attending church regularly; he became a deacon and eventually served twelve years as the chairman of the Deacon Board. Through his efforts and those of his children, Moses had learned to read and write and regularly read Bible scriptures at his church.

When it came time to meet his maker, Moses died a peaceful death. Annie, along with her siblings, helped him to this passing by visiting frequently, telephoning, and writing. Moses showed them how to die. It was a lesson for all of them.

Mamadou was the next to suffer a serious illness. One evening in December 2007, he called Annie about a medical condition that he was experiencing. He said he had developed swelling in his lower extremities and in his genital area. Annie told him some of the causes of the edema and told him that he should seek medical attention. A few days later when Mamadou and Maggie arrived at Helaine's house in Maryland, Helaine took one look at Mamadou and convinced him to go to the emergency room at a nearby hospital. Upon being tested, the attending doctors there told him he was suffering from liver damage and prescribed several different medications for him. Mamadou continued under the care of these doctors in Maryland, even after he went back to MT Union with Maggie. He would make periodic trips to Maryland for treatment. During the course of treatment his doctors told him that he needed a liver transplant. Mamadou was against this. He said, "I want to go out of this world with the same organs that I came into this world with." Mamadou clung to this decision and began to make plans for his death. He was hospitalized and was very sick. Annie flew to Maryland to see him and returned home feeling that perhaps she had seen Mamadou for the last time.

One evening, as Annie lay in bed reading, the phone rang. It was Mamadou. He had all kinds of questions about liver transplants. Annie told him all that she knew about them. At the end of their conversation Mamadou said, "I think I'll go ahead and have the procedure." Annie was happy that he had changed his mind and made plans to return to Maryland to be present for his surgery.

On arrival at the hospital in Maryland, Annie found Mamadou in good spirits. The day before his surgery all of his brothers, sisters, sisters-in-law, brothers-in-law and his mother met in Mamadou's room. His doctors arrived and told them all what to expect. Mamadou told them all that he needed their support to have the surgery and to recover from it. Everyone agreed to give him their support.

On Mamadou's surgical day the above family members, along with several nieces and nephews spent the day in the surgical waiting room while he had his surgery. At about 8PM the chief surgeon came to the waiting room to tell them that Mamadou had survived the surgery and would soon be brought to his room: Several brothers and sisters decided to stay all night to be sure that he was alright. Since Maggie was tired, Annie took her to her hotel room to spend the night. Ben drove them there.

Early the next morning, Annie and Maggie ate breakfast at the hotel and then went to the hospital. The nurses told them that Mamadou had been awake but was now sleeping. He had received medication because he had tried to pull his tubes out. He slept until that evening. He was now rational and in good spirits. Annie stayed two more days and then prepared to fly back to Florida. She kissed Mamadou goodbye, wishing him success in recovering from his surgery.

Since Mamadou was going to be getting an apartment of his own, Jim planned a house warming party for him. Mamadou had stayed with Helaine and then Jim and Shirley when he had been so sick prior to his surgery. Since she had so recently been in Maryland, Annie decided to just send a house warming gift, a comforter, to Mamadou. The party was a success and Mamadou received many gifts.

As the days went on Annie kept in close contact with Mamadou. Things did not go as well as they all expected. Mamadou would call Annie telling her that he was having a lot of trouble walking when he went for his appointments. Annie told him to ask the hospital staff for assistance in pushing him in a wheelchair. She also called other brothers and sisters for help for him and learned that he had already been in touch with them. They were all alarmed when his doctors told him that the Hepatitis C was attacking his new liver and that he was not a candidate for another transplant. He soon got sicker, had more surgery, and then went into a hepatic coma, having all types of tubes and machines connected to him. His brothers and sisters kept a regular vigil in the waiting room outside his room. Helaine called Annie and invited her to join them at his bedside. Annie did just that and spent eight days there taking comfort in being with the rest of the family as they dealt with Mamadou's impending death. His doctors met with the family, telling them what to expect. The family took some ease when the medical staff told them that Mamadou would remain at the hospital until the end. Mamadou had relented and had the surgery. It turned out not to be enough. He was buried the day before Easter in 2009 in MT Union, Pennsylvania near Moses' grave site. Although he was the youngest sibling, he was the first taken. His death was painful for his family, the only comfort being that they dealt with it together. Mamadou had one marriage. It ended in divorce. He also has one daughter Ayanna, who lives in Virginia. His legacy also includes five books and numerous articles.

CHAPTER SIXTY-EIGHT

The next youngest sibling, Jim, was diagnosed with cancer of the pancreas in 2010. After his surgery, he was able to return to his job as a lawyer for the Teamster Union, often going directly to work from his chemotherapy sessions. Jim preferred not to want or need the close attention that Mamadou had received. His marriage of thirty-seven years to Shirley Clair McCall was a close one and with the help of their thirty-two-year-old son, Marcus, they were able to deal with the situation admirably. Nevertheless, his illness worsened in 2011. Shirley was able to take a leave from her job as an administrator in the Washington DC public school system to spend time with Jim as he got sicker. When she or Marcus heeded relief, Shirley called Helaine or Ben for help. They were both retired and were available to stay with Jim. Only later did Helaine tell Annie that Jim and Shirley felt neglected by the family in the last days of his illness. This revelation hurt Annie very much as she had wanted to visit Jim but felt that he, Shirley, and Marcus wanted to deal with the situation alone. Other family members felt the same way. On looking back, Annie wished that she had ignored what she thought was their desire to deal with the situation alone and visited them regardless of what she thought they wanted. Helaine called John and let him know that they wanted visits. So, he and his family did visit. Dorothy was determined that regardless of how they felt, she was going to visit and did so. Annie felt bad especially when she was unable to attend Jim's funeral because of missing her flight and arriving in Washington DC two hours after the funeral. She was able to attend his burial in MT Union, however. After the funeral Ben was pushing Maggie in a wheelchair when she suddenly lost consciousness in what was later deemed a stroke. They were still at the church on the way to the social room for the repast when this all happened. Maggie was hospitalized and after a week was well enough to be discharged.

Maggie returned to MT Union briefly, accompanied by Helaine. When she was not well enough to live alone she was admitted to a nursing home in Lancaster, Pennsylvania near Janelle's home. She eventually had another stroke and died in March 2012, surrounded by Janelle and Maggie's grandchildren. Ander, being one of the grandchildren present, telephoned Annie to tell her of Maggie's passing. Her funeral was held in MT Union and she was buried next to Moses in their adjoining plot.

Three months later in June of 2012, Rod, John's oldest son, was stabbed to death in a bar where he had gone after work. Of course, the whole family was devastated by his death at the age of 41 years. He was six months younger than Ander and they had always been close. Annie made two trips North that year. One to help funeralize her mother and two, to give what consolation she could to her brother, sister-in-law, and their two younger children, at the death of Rod.

Eugenia Ann, (Gena), Dorothy's oldest daughter and one of her twins, was the next to go. She was diagnosed with colon cancer in 2012. Although she recovered enough to work from home for the Social Security Administration, she succumbed to the disease in 2014. Gena left to mourn her husband of ten years, Eddie, and their little boy, Taylor, age 6 years, along with other relatives and friends.

Dorothy was hospitalized in the summer of 2014, complaining of abdominal and back pain. After multiple tests, she, like Jim, received a diagnosis of pancreatic cancer. Dorothy refused any type of surgery and was treated with chemotherapy, initially, doing well with it and even gaining some weight. She was unable to tolerate much food, however, and soon began to fail. Dorothy's main goal, in light of her illness, was to find suitable care for her husband, Broadus, who had suffered from Alzheimer's disease for many years. She was successful and as she declined, they were both being cared for in a private home by an aide and her husband. On some days, Broadus would come into Dorothy's room and feed her. She and Broadus were fortunate enough to have three remaining children who were devoted to them. When their oldest daughter, Valerie, contacted Ander two days in a row, Annie knew that the children needed help dealing with Dorothy's impeding death, causing her and Ander to visit Dorothy and Broadus for five days. Their visit was well received not only by the children but also by Helaine and Ben, who lived nearby and visited them daily. While Annie and Ander visited over the Mother's Day weekend 2015, Helaine held a cookout at her home for the extended family.

Annie and Dorothy had always been close, there being only one year between them. When Helaine called to tell Annie of Dorothy's passing, she felt a profound sense of loss and although expecting Helaine's call, she burst into tears. She flew back to Maryland for Dorothy's funeral, in order to lend what support she could to Dorothy's children, grandchildren and Broadus.

CHAPTER SIXTY-NINE

Visiting Dorothy during her impeding death and seeing how bravely she faced her death and how she prevented her children from being overwhelmed by doing as much of the planning as she could, inspired Annie to begin to prepare for her eventual death. After all, she was approaching seventy-eight and she could possibly be a victim of cancer, since it was affecting so many family members. She did not want to leave everything to Ander. Thus Annie contacted a nearby funeral director and with the help of his staff, put the wheels in motion for how she wanted her funeral and burial to be carried out. She planned the program for the funeral even designating who was to give the eulogy and which of her neices and nephews she wanted to sing, and what songs to sing. She prepared an article for the newspapers and wrote out an obituary. She sent her youngest sister, Janelle, a copy of the program and made sure that Ander knew where to find important papers. In the past when Annie tried to discuss her death with Ander, he always resisted and would not discuss it with her. Now, he agreed to sit with Annie when she met with the funeral home staff. He did remind Annie, however, that it was entirely possible that he could proceed her in death and told her how he wanted his funeral to be. Ander, on visiting his Aunt Dorothy and standing there while she discussed her death with him, seemed to make more real the possibility of his mother's passing, as well as his own eventual demise. Annie agreed to carry out his wishes in the case of him proceeding her in death, the most important being the necessity of having a Muslim funeral and being buried in a Muslim cemetery, the one near Orlando, Florida next to Margo, his late wife.

CHAPTER SEVENTY

At the present time Annie leads a quiet but full life residing on the southwest coast of Florida right on the Gulf of Mexico in a single-family dwelling. Being a night owl, she arises at approximately 9:30AM each morning and has breakfast, while watching the morning news. She spends the middle part of the day studying the Word and writing. Next, Annie swims for one half hour, then relaxes in her hot tub, enjoying the usual balmy Florida weather. Ander lives ten minutes away and usually pops in sometime during the day. When Annie does not feel up to it, Ander helps her out by doing the laundry and cleaning the house.

Along with her other illnesses, Annie also suffers from osteoarthritis. DR Steven Chun diagnosed her as having degenerative disc disease (DDD). Along with treating Annie with the morphine pump, DR Chun also periodically does facet oblation of spinal nerves which are being pinched by the degenerated discs. The osteoarthritis also causes destruction of the cartilage in the joints in some of Annie's extremities. In 2010, she began having severe pain in her right knee and after treatments of cortisone injections having minimal effect, had surgery on that knee with a knee replacement.

Although Annie leads a rather sheltered life in Florida, she cannot help but empathize with people like "The Mothers of the Movement" (as shown during the Democratic National Convention in 2016). She shares their grief especially when circumstances such as the death of Iddy occurs. She wishes she could do more to alleviate some of the problems in the inner cities of America. In Iddy's case, Annie and Ander did what they could to help him: He spent summers during some of his teenage years with Annie. Ander wanted him to move with him in 2012 when he relocated to Florida. Iddy refused saying, "It's too boring down there." The money that Annie was keeping for him until he decided to go to school, she sent to Shameika for his funeral. Ander also sent money.

Ander has lived long enough to make wise decisions in his choices of where to live and where to socialize. He realizes that to live in the inner cities would increase the chance of an early death. Therefore, he moved to Florida and when he bought property he chose a house in a mixed neighborhood. These actions were the direct result of his mother's advice over the years. Annie remembers that when she was deciding to move to Florida, Ander advised her to move to a "Black" neighborhood. She jokingly asked him if he would want to be in a "Black" area of Heaven.

Without a doubt there are racial problems in America. They must be solved together. Most of Annie's ancestors came to this country not of their own choosing. Some of the problems here are a direct result of that fact. Genocide among Native Americans also occurred and has caused many problems. However we cannot wallow in these occurrences. We must as a group take measures to overcome them. Education is one of the means to that end. There must be more attention and funds directed there. When Annie has needed to hire such skilled workmen as plumbers, electricians, or air conditioner repairmen, she notices that in many cases the mostly white contractors bring an apprentice with them. These apprentices are always white. This practice ensures that the next generation of these skilled workers will also be white with white apprentices. This eliminates the possibility of any Blacks making it in these fields. There must be changes made if there are ever going to be any inroads into these professions for young Black men. Community colleges and state universities have made it possible for Blacks to enter many professions. The same way that these institutions have made it possible for Blacks to enter many professions must be studied and ways developed to ensure Black entry in the skilled workman fields. Together we can solve this and any other problem that shuts out a group of people from any particular line of work. The same ways that were instituted to ensure people of all races being able to become teachers, health care workers, and social workers can be developed to help Blacks enter the skilled workman field.

These and other issues occupy Annie's thoughts as she goes about her daily routine of swimming, computing, and attending church on Sundays and occasionally during the week. Although Annie attends and is a member of a Southern Baptist church, she is presently writing proposals for grants in an attempt, along with her son and several of his Muslim brothers to secure funds to build an Islamic mosque for Manatee County, as the closest mosque is twenty-five miles away. A mosque is sorely needed as Muslims pray five times a day, preferably at the mosque. Upon relocating to Bradenton, Ander founded a mosque there and maintained it for three years until he had a relapse of his illness, upon which time the mosque closed, although it was utilized by approximately fifty individuals.

The above activities plus others keep Annie's life relevant and meaningful. She believes along with Peter that "His divine power has given us everything we need for a godly life through our knowledge of Him who called us by his own glory and goodness." 2 Peter 1:3

Made in the USA
Columbia, SC
29 August 2021